Building on the American Heritage Series

Study Guide

Building on the American Heritage Series Study Guide

1st Edition, 1st Printing, July 2016

Additional materials available from
WallBuilders
P. O. Box 397
Aledo, Texas 76008
817-441-6044
WallBuilders.com

Cover Image
The Supreme Council, 330, Southern Jurisdiction, Washington, D. C.

Design
Joshua Russell

ISBN 10: 1-932225-96-X
ISBN 13: 978-1-932225-96-9

Printed in the United States of America

TABLE OF CONTENTS

PRESERVING AMERICA'S HERITAGE

"The highest glory of the American Revolution was this: it connected in one indissoluble bond the principles of civil government with the principles of Christianity."

— John Quincy Adams

PRESERVING AMERICA'S HERITAGE

INTRODUCTION

Is America a Christian nation? What does that mean? And why does it matter?

Today, many people believe that we are not and should not be a Christian nation. After all, we may be Christians, but we certainly don't want to exclude those from other faiths — we cherish America's "freedom of religion." Does this then mean that we should not be a Christian nation? Are religion and government never to mix? Interestingly, those who embrace this view have a wrong understanding of what it really means to be a Christian nation.

In this session, you'll learn that the Founders (as well as generations before and after them) defined a "Christian nation" very differently than we do today. To them, America was a Christian nation because its institutions, customs, and culture had been shaped by the Bible and its teachings. This was the historic definition of a Christian nation, and it was affirmed by many Supreme Court, federal court, and state court decisions, as well as by numerous presidents, congresses, and other national leaders. But today, the traditional meaning of a Christian nation has been redefined to be something negative and exclusionary rather than something positive and uplifting.

And as we have become an increasingly secular nation, we embrace and apply the Bible and its teachings less and less. The result is that we find the historic institutions of our country (such as education, law, economics, government, and so forth) increasingly diminishing in effectiveness and our culture sinking lower and lower into selfishness, immorality, meanness, and debauchery. Now more than ever it's important to return to the Biblical teachings that shaped our national institutions — the teachings that caused America to become the most prosperous and free nation in history.

This session explores:

- How the Bible influenced our institutions and the structure of our government
- Why sound education is necessary to preserve freedom
- How Christianity provides protection for all religions
- Why Christians should be involved in the civic arena
- Why civil disobedience is sometimes a Biblical duty

 DISCUSSION QUESTIONS BEFORE WATCHING THE VIDEO

1. What does it mean to be a "Christian nation?"
2. Does the Bible address how government should work?
3. What does "render to Caesar" mean to us today?

Are we a Christian nation?

In 1892, the U. S. Supreme Court delivered a unanimous ruling affirming previous court decisions that America was indeed a Christian nation. Justice David Brewer (*1837-1910*), who penned the Court's ruling, later wrote a book expounding on what it means to be a Christian nation. He first addressed what a Christian nation is not (which, interestingly, is what many today now wrongly believe that it is):

> [I]n what sense can [America] be called a Christian nation? Not in the sense that Christianity is the established religion, or that the people are in any manner compelled to support it. On the contrary, the Constitution specifically provides that "Congress shall make no law respecting an establishment of religion, or prohibiting the free exercise thereof." Neither is it Christian in the sense that all its citizens are either in fact or name Christians.

1

SESSION

STUDY GUIDE

> On the contrary, all religions have free scope within our borders. Numbers of our people profess other religions, and many reject all. Nor is it Christian in the sense that a profession of Christianity is a condition of holding office or otherwise engaging in public service, or essential to recognition either politically or socially. In fact, the government as a legal organization is independent of all religions. Nevertheless, we constantly speak of this republic as a Christian nation — in fact, as the leading Christian nation of the world.

THEOCRACY
A government run by an individual or a group not elected by the people and which claims to be the immediate representative of God and act directly on His behest.

So... a Christian nation is not one filled only with Christians, nor does it give exclusive rights or privileges to Christians. It is not a theocracy, and it does not utilize coercion. These are the things that Americans today have been wrongly told are associated with being a Christian nation.

So if all of this is not what a Christian nation is, then what is a Christian nation? What is its proper definition? According to Justice Brewer, America is "most justly called a Christian nation" because Christianity "so largely shaped and molded it." The historic definition of a Christian nation is a nation that has been largely shaped and molded by Christianity.

REPUBLIC
A government in which supreme power resides in the people at large, who from time to time elect officials to represent them in governing and making laws, with those officials being accountable to the people and governed by the laws they make. An elective government cannot be a Theocracy.

1. The Bible changed the way we run government.

The Christian Pilgrims who came over on the Mayflower refused to set up either a Monarchy or a Theocracy, which were common forms of government in their day. Instead they set up a representative government where leaders in both church and state were elected by the people every year. It was Christianity and the Bible that produced our cherished republican form of government, where citizens can choose their own leaders. (See verses such as Exodus 18:21 and Deuteronomy 1:15, 16:18.)

Additionally, America has a written constitution. But this is not because we inherited this practice from Great Britain, for even to this day the British still do not have a written constitution. We have a written constitution because that's the example that God gave in the Scriptures: He delivered a written law to His people and a written code to govern the nation. This provided national stability, because everyone could then know exactly what the laws were, for they were fixed, written in black and white; in fact, some were even written in stone!

2. The Bible caused us to be a benevolent nation.

The extensive and pervasive influence of Christianity on our country is also evident in our civil laws, and especially in the attitudes that caused these laws to be passed. For example, a Good Samaritan law is found on the books of most states, but the story of the Good Samaritan on which these laws are based is found only within Christianity.

> *"Then Jesus answered and said: 'A certain man went down from Jerusalem to Jericho, and fell among thieves, who stripped him of his clothing, wounded him, and departed, leaving him half dead....But a certain Samaritan, as he journeyed, came where he was. And when he saw him, he had compassion. So he went to him and bandaged his wounds, pouring on oil and wine..."*
>
> – Luke 10: 29-37

> *"...the teachings of the Bible are so interwoven and entwined with our whole civic and social life that it would be literally — I do not mean figuratively, I mean literally — impossible for us to figure to ourselves what the life would be if these teachings were removed."*
>
> — Theodore Roosevelt

South Carolina Good Samaritan Law, Section 15-1-310.
Any person who in good faith gratuitously renders emergency care at the scene of an accident or emergency to the victim thereof, shall not be liable for any civil damages for any personal injury as a result of any act or omission by such person in rendering the emergency care...

The Golden Rule, another Christian teaching, also forms the basis for much public policy and has been regularly referred to as an authority in American court decisions.

> *"So whatever you wish that others would do to you, do also to them, for this is the Law and the Prophets."*
>
> – Matthew 7:12

Both the teaching of the Good Samaritan and the Golden Rule are representative of the numerous Bible teachings instructing us to help those in need; and we are to help them whether we know them or not, and regardless of whether they are friends or enemies. These Bible teachings that have shaped the character of our nation routinely cause America to be the first on the scene to provide help and relief whenever foreign nations suffer devastation, natural disasters, or other ravages.

For example, when the largest Muslim nation in the world, Indonesia, was hit by a tsunami in 2004, the other Muslim nations barely responded. But Christian America was quickly on the scene, providing massive amounts of humanitarian aid. This was also true following the devastating earthquakes in Mexico and Haiti, the cyclone in Bangladesh, mudslides in Brazil, and so many other disasters. The Bible teachings on benevolence were deeply embedded in our public policy and national fabric — one of the many indications that America is indeed a Christian nation according to the historic definition.

3. Our free market system came from the Bible.

History affirms that those who originally implemented and gradually developed America's free-market/free-enterprise relied on the principles set forth in Scriptures such as:

- 1 Timothy 5:8
- 2 Thessalonians 3:10
- Luke 19:11-27
- Matthew 20:1-16
- Matthew 25:14-30

Today, many academics identify Scottish economist Adam Smith as the "Father of Modern Economics" or the "Father of Capitalism" because of his 1776 work *Wealth of Nations*. While this is an excellent treatise addressing the free-market system, that system, based on Biblical principles, largely existed in America for decades before Smith's book was written. And before Smith wrote *The Wealth of Nations*, he had penned *The Theory of Moral Sentiments*, setting forth the Christian morality that must exist before a successful free-market economic system can function properly and efficiently. If there is no Biblical morality undergirding business, then what keeps a mechanic from claiming that he has changed your oil and collecting money when in reality he did nothing? Or what prevents a waiter from spitting in food he prepares for you before he brings it from the kitchen to the table? Biblical morality is indispensable to the successful operation of a free-market economic system.

Significantly, for centuries all Americans, both Christians and non-Christians, were taught a Biblical morality — a fact demonstrated by Founding Father Thomas Paine, one of only a handful of Founders who was actually anti-Christian. Paine claimed that his non-religious life displayed honorable character traits often associated with true Christians, such as honor, integrity, truthfulness, fidelity, and so forth, but Benjamin Franklin pointedly reminded him:

> [Y]ou are indebted to her originally, that is, to your religious education, for the habits of virtue upon which you now justly value yourself.

While Paine might not have been religious as an adult, he certainly had been raised learning Christian morality and character values, and thus the fundamental differences between right and wrong. The entire nation, including non-Christians, long embraced and benefitted from Biblical moral standards, which are the basis of a healthy and strong Biblically-derived free-market economic system — yet another indication that America is indeed an historic Christian nation.

> *"...to manufacture for themselves, or use colony manufactures only [i.e., the free market system], be the means, under God, of recovering and establishing the freedom of our country entire, and of handing it down complete to our posterity."*
> — Benjamin Franklin

4. Our education system was founded because of the Bible.

The first public school law (1647) was passed to ensure that people could read the Scriptures. Those who enacted that law explained that it is only when citizens know the Bible and its teachings that they can restrain oppressive government and confine it to its proper role.

So firmly was American education rooted in Christian principles, that by 1860, of the 246 colleges in America, only 17 of them had not been founded by churches, Christians, or denominations; and ninety-one percent of college presidents were ministers of the Gospel — as were more than a third of all university faculty members. So both public and university education were the product of Christianity and the Bible — another indication that America, according to the historic definition, is indeed a Christian nation.

(By the way, when America still maintained religious elements throughout its public education system, we were #1 in the world in literacy; but in 1962 after the Supreme Court mandated secular public education and the removal of Christian principles, we fell to #65 in the world.)

1 SESSION

STUDY GUIDE

5. We protect the rights of religious conscience, which means we practice religious toleration and non-coercion.

A true Christian nation not only is not coercive but it also allows individuals to make their own choices concerning their faith and religious conscience.

The old Christian nations of Europe were coercive largely because they were not Biblical. For almost 1,000 years, those so-called Christian nations forbid common people from having access to the Bible. They forced all people to practice a state-determined version of Christianity, even mandating which churches citizens must attend and the particular doctrines to which they must adhere. Violations resulted in penalties up to and including death. But the arrival of the Reformation and its emphasis on returning to the Bible eventually restored religious freedom.

America was formed with a strong reliance on Biblical Reformation teachings rather than state-decreed doctrines. Consequently, as early as 1636, government documents written in America specifically protected the rights of religious conscience — the right to choose one's religion and how to practice it. This became a common feature of American governmental documents over the next century-and-a-half — just the opposite of Europe's non-Biblical state-established coercive "Christianity." But it is not surprising that those in America who relied so heavily on the Bible should craft their public policies to protect the rights of conscience, for there are some 30 verses in the New Testament addressing the importance of conscience, and several stress the importance of protecting the rights of religious conscience.

"But when you thus sin against the brethren, and wound their weak conscience, you sin against Christ."

– 1 Corinthians 8:12

ADDITIONAL RESOURCE
Four Centuries of American Education
by David Barton

STUDY GUIDE

SESSION 1

America's implementation of Christian teachings on religious toleration, non-coercion, and protecting the rights of conscience are demonstrated in many ways even today. For example:

#1. Quakers are not required to serve in the military because to do so would violate their sincerely held religious beliefs.

#2. Jews and Muslims who wear beards for religious reasons may keep them, regardless of what business dress codes may require.

#3. The compulsory 12-year education law for American students is not applied to Amish, for their religious beliefs hold that a child should be taught formal education for only 8 years.

#4. The legal requirement to say the Pledge of Allegiance in schools is suspended for Jehovah's Witnesses, whose religious beliefs require they pledge allegiance to no one but God.

#5. Mandatory vaccinations for school children are not required for Christian Scientists, whose religious teachings forbid that procedure.

So, the national protection for the rights of conscience for all faiths is the direct product of Christian/Biblical teachings and is yet another indication that by historic definitions, America is indeed a Christian nation.

Question #1: Why should I, as a Christian, be involved in government when my main focus under the Great Commission is to share the Gospel?

A. It is an errant view of Scripture which asserts that a choice must be made between government and God. To the contrary, Jesus specifically declared:

> ***"Render therefore to Caesar the things that are Caesar's, and to God the things that are God's."***
>
> — Matthew 22:21

In this Scripture, Jesus does not say Caesar "or" God, rather He says Caesar "and" God — that is, we have a civil duty to fulfill and we have a spiritual duty to fulfill.

STUDY GUIDE

Furthermore, in the Great Commission (Matthew 28:18-20), Jesus did not say "Go evangelize the world." Rather, He said "Go, make disciples" and "teach them everything I have taught you." So what are some of the things that Jesus taught, which we are also to teach others?

- Matthew 19:1-10: No-fault divorce is wrong; the definition of marriage is the lifelong union of one man and one woman.
- Matthew 20:1-16: The inviolability of contracts between employers and employees; contracts are to be made without government interference; there should be no minimum wage.
- Matthew 25:14-30: Profit-makers should be rewarded, not penalized, and thus taxes such as the capital gains tax are wrong.

These are only a few of the many teachings which Jesus delivered that we are to teach others — teachings that have direct application to government and public policy. So if we fulfill the Great Commission, then we must directly address such areas related to civil governance.

B. God gives us the right — indeed, God mandates — that we are to share the Gospel with all people in all nations. But sadly, not all nations provide political protection for that God-given right, and persecution occurs whenever political protection is not extended for the exercise of a God-given right. For example, try to exercise your God-given right to preach the Gospel in Saudi Arabia or Iran. The lack of political protection in a country for any God-given right occurs when citizens do not place God-fearing and Biblical-minded leaders in office.

C. We are to "render to Caesar," but who is "Caesar" in America — who is "the government" in our country? We are. Our Constitution declares that the supreme authority in America is "We The People." So when Jesus says to "render to Caesar what is Caesar's," in our form of government, He is actually telling us to go do our part and be a good and active steward of our government rather than stay away from it.

Question #2: Isn't God going to pick the rulers regardless of whether I'm involved or voting in the election?

The Bible tells us in multiple locations that God does indeed ordain the institution of government (see verses such as Romans 13:1-7, I Peter 2:13-14, I Timothy 1:8-10, I Timothy 2:1-3, Titus 3:1, and others). So what type of government has God ordained in America? Self-government. Therefore, God has ordained a form of government of which we are in charge — He has put the government into our hands. We cannot sit on the sidelines and still be good stewards of what He has given us. If we neglect the great institutions we enjoy in America and give them over to people with unBiblical views, then we will answer to God as well as to subsequent generations.

We can't look at government as if we are merely transient travelers, just passing through, soon to leave this world. To the contrary, Jesus explicitly commands, "Occupy till I come" (Luke 19:13). It is a faulty theology that teaches that we are not to be salt or light, but only to prepare for His soon coming. Every generation since Christ was on earth more than 2,000 years ago believed that He would return in their generation, and so far they have all been wrong. He definitely will return, but it will be in His time; and as He told His disciples, He doesn't even know when that will be (Mark 13:32). So until then, we are to occupy — we are to move forward and press into, not back away from.

God has put into our hands the responsibility of choosing our rulers, and we are told in passages such as Exodus 18:21 and Proverbs 29:2 just what type of leaders we should select. If we don't obey Him and select the type of leaders He has indicated, then we will have deliberately and voluntarily handed our government over to pagans, who will transform American into an entirely different nation from what God intends.

"...to God and posterity you are accountable for [your rights and your rulers]...Let not your children have reason to curse you for giving up those rights and prostrating those institutions which your fathers delivered to you."
— Matthias Burnet, preached at Hartford on the day of the Anniversary Election, May 21st, 1803

"I hope you will have good sense enough to disregard those foolish predictions that the world is to be at an end soon. The Almighty has never made known to any body at what time He created it; nor will He tell to any body when He will put an end to it, if He ever means to do it. As to preparations for that event, the best way is for you always to be prepared for it...."
— Thomas Jefferson in a letter to his daughter

Question #3: Doesn't the Bible say to submit to authority, and not to disagree?

A. The Bible does say to submit to proper God-ordained authority, but it definitely doesn't say to remain silent and not to disagree or stand up for what is right. In fact, many of the heroes of our Christian faith listed in Hebrews 11 openly disobeyed civil authority. Daniel did so (Daniel 6:1-13), as did the three Hebrew children (Daniel 3:1-18), the Apostles (Acts 4:19-20, 5:29), the Hebrew midwives (Exodus 1:15-17), and many others. All of these courageous champions directly disobeyed unjust civil authority and were honored by God for doing so.

In passages such as Romans 13, we are commanded to submit to the general institution of government, but that does not mean to every specific individual government. As a corollary, we know that God has ordained the institution of the Church, but that does not mean that He has ordained every specific church that exists, for many churches teach exactly the opposite of what His Word teaches. God has similarly ordained the institution of the family, but that does not mean that every family is ordained of God, for many families are formed in direct disobedience to what God commanded families to be and do. So, too, with government.

God ordained the institution of government, and we are to submit to the institution — we are not to live in anarchy; but this does not mean we must submit to every specific government or government policy that has been instituted. Whenever the civil government commands us to do something that violates what God has commanded, we always have a duty to disobey government and obey God's higher law instead (see Acts 4:19-20, 5:29).

B. So, are we to submit to government? Yes — when it is not contradicting Biblical commands. But also remember that in America, we are the governmental authority. Our leaders are actually our servants and substitutes — they are accountable to us in their offices. We are the masters, they are the servants, not vice versa.

> ***The order of things in Britain is exactly the reverse of the order of things in the United States. Here, the people are masters of the government: there, the government is master of the people.***
>
> – James Wilson

C. We have a Biblical duty to use our voice.

The Bible tells us that the reason Moses was not allowed to enter the Promised Land was that he disobeyed God. We also learn that because Aaron remained silent and inactive during that incident of disobedience by Moses, God also did not allow Aaron to enter the Promised Land. The Scripture clearly tells us that if we remain silent when we should speak, then God will impute to us the very sin that we did not confront and call out (see Ezekiel 3:17-21, 33:2-9).

> ***"Deliver those who are drawn toward death, and hold back those stumbling to the slaughter. If you say, 'Surely we did not know this,' does not He who weighs the hearts consider it? He who keeps your soul, does He not know it? And will He not render to each man according to his deeds?"***
>
> — Proverbs 24:11-12

> ***"When I [God] say to the wicked, 'You wicked person, you will surely die,' and you do not speak out to dissuade them from their ways, that wicked person will die for their sin, and I will hold you accountable for their blood."***
>
> — Ezekiel 3:17, 33:8

When we see unrighteousness being advanced in policies and we fail to speak out, then we will have to give account to God for our silence and our refusal to be involved.

> Constitution of Massachusetts, Part the First, Article V:
> *"All power residing originally in the people, and being derived from them, the several magistrates and officers of government, vested with authority, whether legislative, executive, or judicial, are their substitutes and agents, and are at all times accountable to them."*

 ADDITIONAL READING/VIEWING/LISTENING

- *America's Godly Heritage* by David Barton
- *The Influence of the Bible on America* by David Barton
- *The Role of Pastors and Christians in Civil Government* by David Barton
- "The American Revolution: Was it an Act of Biblical Rebellion?" at WallBuilders.com
- *The Spirit of the American Revolution* by David Barton

1 SESSION

STUDY GUIDE

★ DISCUSSION QUESTIONS AFTER WATCHING THE VIDEO

1. Why does it matter whether or not we are a Christian nation?

The freedoms, institutions, and blessings we enjoy, such as the right to follow our own conscience, the ability to start a business, the widespread opportunities for education, and so much else is produced by Christian principles. If we remove these Christian influences, America will not be the same free and prosperous nation she has been, and all citizens — both Christian and non-Christian — will suffer the negative results of this absence.

2. Am I allowing my view of the end times to unconsciously breed apathy or provide an excuse for non-involvement in myself and others?

(Discuss your actions or lack thereof caused by your view of the end times)

3. What are some ways we can be involved in keeping our government accountable?

- Stay informed about issues and how well they comport with Biblical teachings
- Vote — and vote for candidates who most closely represent Biblical beliefs and values
- Attend local school board/county council meetings
- Call your leaders and voice your opinions and concerns
- Donate to a good candidate, or help with their campaign
- Recruit good people to run for office, or run for a local office yourself
- Educate others — use the influence you have to inform and involve others (social media, individual conversations, personal newsletters, etc.)

Session 2

FOUNDATIONS OF AMERICAN GOVERNMENT

"The God Who gave us life, gave us liberty at the same time. The hand of force may destroy, but cannot disjoin them."

— Thomas Jefferson

FOUNDATIONS OF AMERICAN GOVERNMENT

INTRODUCTION

Is America truly exceptional? Is the unusual stability and prosperity we've enjoyed just a happy accident? If not, then what is the secret of America's unprecedented longevity and stability?

America's government rests on five simple but profound principles found in the Declaration of Independence. They were not just five random ideas but were Bible-based teachings that revolutionized popular thinking about man and government and the responsibility of each.

The exceptionalism produced by the five principles from the Declaration is under attack today from those who want to separate freedom from its religious foundation. This is why it is imperative that Americans understand the principles that produced the longest ongoing constitutional republic in the history of the world as well as the many blessings we still enjoy today as a result of applying those principles.

In today's session, you'll learn:

- The five principles that make a successful government
- The difference between a democracy and a republic, and why it matters
- The proper role of "the consent of the governed" and majority rule
- The importance of the Declaration of Independence to modern government
- The positive impact of the Bible on the Constitution

DISCUSSION QUESTIONS BEFORE WATCHING THE VIDEO

1. Does the two-century old Declaration of Independence have any practical importance or application for us today? If so, what?
2. Is America a republic or a democracy? What does each mean?
3. Why do we need civil government? What is its purpose?

What is the cause of America's success?

The five principles that produced America's stability and prosperity are found in 126 words from the Declaration of Independence.

When in the course of human events, it becomes necessary for one people to dissolve the political bands which have connected them with another, and to assume among the powers of the earth, the separate and equal station to which the Laws of Nature and of Nature's God entitle them, a decent respect to the opinions of mankind requires that they should declare the causes which impel them to the separation. We hold these truths to be self-evident, that all men are created equal, that they are endowed by their Creator with certain unalienable rights, that among these are life, liberty and the pursuit of happiness.--That to secure these rights, governments are instituted among men, deriving their just powers from the consent of the governed.

Principle #1. The public acknowledgment of a Divine Creator. ("We hold these truths to be self-evident, that all men are created equal . . .")

The first step in having a limited government is to openly recognize that there is a Power greater than the government — a Power to Whom even government itself must answer. A secular government routinely tries to assume the role of God and become the supreme and intimate force in the lives of citizens. But a government that openly acknowledges God recognizes that a limitation has been placed on its power, and that it is to serve the people rather than vice versa.

Today, we are routinely told that government is to be neutral between religion and non-religion — that it must be religion-free so as not to offend the anti-religious. But that is not what the Declaration declares or what the Founding Fathers avowed was to be America's public policy. For example,

2 SESSION

STUDY GUIDE

> "And can the liberties of a nation be thought secure when we have removed their only firm basis: a conviction in the minds of the people that these liberties are of the gift of God? — That they are not to be violated but with His wrath? Indeed I tremble for my country when I reflect that God is just, that His justice cannot sleep forever."
> — Thomas Jefferson

George Washington affirmed that governments are openly to acknowledge the Divine Creator:

> It is the duty of all nations to acknowledge the Providence of Almighty God, to obey His will, to be grateful for His benefits, and humbly to implore His protection and favor.

The open acknowledgement of God by civil government is the first of the five principles in the philosophy that made America so unique and great.

Principle #2. The Creator gives certain inalienable rights to every individual. ("...all men are created equal, that they are endowed by their Creator with certain unalienable rights...")

American government begins with the official acknowledgement that there is a Creator, and secondly recognizes that the Creator gives inalienable rights to every individual. What is an "inalienable right"? Constitution signer John Dickinson said that it was a right "which God gave to you and which no inferior power has a right to take away." He explained that these rights come to us "from the King of kings, and Lord of all the earth... They are born with us; exist with us; and cannot be taken from us by any human power."

John Adams said that inalienable rights are "antecedent to all earthly government; rights that cannot be repealed or restrained by human laws; rights derived from the Great Legislator of the Universe."

Other Founding Fathers stated the same — that inalienable rights are those rights specifically bestowed on man by the Creator Himself, and not by any human power or through the act of any civil government. Every human being receives these rights from the Creator simply by virtue of his existence, without regard to ethnicity, gender, or geographic distinction.

The Declaration of Independence tells us that our inalienable rights include the right to life, liberty, and private property, and the Bill of Rights further enumerates inalienable rights such as that of the right to worship God according to the dictates of conscience as well as the right of self-defense, a secure home, justice in courts, and others. And because all of these rights come from God and not man, human government is therefore not allowed to interfere with or regulate these rights. This principle is the second step in limiting government: declaring that certain things are off limits to the jurisdiction of government because these things come from God, not man.

Principle #3. Government exists first and foremost for the purpose of protecting inalienable rights. ("That to secure these rights, governments are instituted among men . . .")

Samuel Adams affirmed, "Government... was originally designed for the preservation of the unalienable rights." And James Wilson, a signer of both the Declaration of Independence and the Constitution, agreed, stating that government was instituted "to acquire a new security for... those rights to... which we were previously entitled by the immediate gift, or by the unerring law of our all-wise and all-beneficent Creator."

The primary purpose of government is not to provide jobs or a strong economy or national healthcare or any other laudable goal but is instead, first and foremost, to ensure that every individual has the right to freely practice his God-given rights without penalty or interference.

Principle #4. There is a fixed moral law. ("... the Laws of Nature and of Nature's God...")

This phrase in the Declaration was derived from the most famous law book of that day — the legal commentaries of William Blackstone. This eight-word phrase represented the dual revelation of God delineated in the Scriptures.

According to Romans 1, everything that can be made known about God, including the intricacies of the Godhead (v. 20), are revealed through what God created (see also Psalms 19:1-4 and 46:10.). Thus, the first revelation of God to man is found in His creation in nature, which tells us

2 SESSION

STUDY GUIDE

many things about what is right and wrong in God's eyes. These are "the laws of nature." These laws affirm the right to life, to freedom, to self-defense, and they likewise confirm the wrongness of homosexuality and abortion (i.e., no species in nature kills its young while still in the womb, and homosexuality is not only extremely rare in nature but it is never a lifestyle and is always an aberration even in these few species where it does occasionally appear).

But after man sinned in the Garden and fell, his understanding became darkened. No longer did he see and understand God's will through creation with the clarity he had before sin entered. So God, in His compassion for man's frailty, gave him His written word, which sets forth in unequivocal terms what God considers to be right and wrong. This written word — the Bible (which the Founders called the Revealed, or Divine Law) — is the law of the God Who created nature; that is, the Bible contains "the laws of nature's God."

"The laws of nature and of nature's God" set forth God's will for man as made clear both in nature and the Scriptures. These two revelations provide a fixed moral standard of what is right and wrong for all mankind.

> ***"For since the creation of the world His invisible attributes are clearly seen, being understood by the things that are made, even His eternal power and Godhead, so that they are without excuse."***
>
> – Romans 1:20

"Man, considered as a creature, must necessarily be subject to the laws of his Creator... ...This will of his Maker is called the law of nature... ...This law of nature... ...is of course superior in obligation to any other. It is binding over all the globe in all countries, and at all times: no human laws are of any validity, if contrary to this... ...[D]ivine Providence... ...has been pleased...to discover and enforce Its laws by an immediate and direct revelation. The doctrines thus delivered we call the revealed or divine law, and they are to be found only in the Holy Scriptures... ... Upon these two foundations, the law of nature and the law of revelation, depend all human laws; that is to say, no human laws should be suffered to contradict these."
— William Blackstone, *Commentaries on the Laws of England*, Volume I

Principle #5. The consent of the governed. (". . . deriving their just powers from the consent of the governed.")

The "consent of the governed" is also called "majority rule." George Washington affirmed that this is a "fundamental principle of our Constitution, which enjoins [requires] that the will of the majority shall prevail." Thomas Jefferson agreed, declaring that "the will of the majority — the natural law of every society — is the only sure guardian of the rights of man."

But the will of the majority (i.e., the consent of the governed) applies only to things below the level of inalienable rights and the fixed moral law.

We can vote (and the majority will then decide) on issues such as how wide sidewalks should be, what the speed limit is, and how much of a fee will be paid for a particular license. But we are not to vote on whether or not we will allow self-defense, for that is a right given to every individual by God Himself. Similarly, we cannot vote on whether rape is right or wrong, for "the laws of nature and of nature's God" already tell us that it is wrong.

The right of the people to vote on everything, including on rights and morals — that is, a government where everything is run by "the consent of the governed" — is a democracy. This is a form of government which our Founders vehemently opposed.

> ***Remember democracy never lasts long. It soon wastes, exhausts, and murders itself. There never was a democracy yet that did not commit suicide.***
>
> – John Adams

> ***[D]emocracies have ever been spectacles of turbulence and contention have ever been found incompatible with personal security or the rights of property and have in general been as short in their lives as they have been violent in their deaths.***
>
> – James Madison

Numerous other Founders made similarly virulent denunciations against democracies.

America is not a democracy, and the Constitution requires that we always remain a republic, which means that the people elect leaders to represent us, and that there are certain things on which no one votes. In a constitutional republic such as America's, our elective government is based on fixed laws rather than transient opinions, which John Adams described as "a government of laws and not of men."

There are four types of law found in the Bible:

- Ceremonial Law — this establishes the means by which someone becomes righteous (but this is no longer applicable for New Testament Christians, for they are made righteous through their personal relationship with Jesus Christ)

2 SESSION

STUDY GUIDE

- Judicial Law — specifies the penalties applied to a crime, and it can change across time
- Moral Law — this is what God says is absolutely right and wrong (such as in the Ten Commandments), and it does not change across time
- Social Compact Law — these are "consent of the governed" laws created by citizens to govern themselves outside the areas of Inalienable Rights and the Moral Law.

Some say that for everyone to be able to do what they want to do is the American idea of freedom, but it is actually moral and political anarchy. Liberty is not the absence of law but rather is the result of having sound law in accord with God's principles.

> ***"In those days there was no king in Israel; everyone did what was right in his own eyes."***
>
> — Judges 17:6

> ***"But one who looks intently at the perfect law, the law of liberty, and abides by it... this man will be blessed in what he does."***
>
> — James 1:25

Question #1: Why do we need government?

God established three human institutions and did so in this order:

- Family
- Civil Government
- Church

Concerning civil government and civil law, the Bible tells us:

> ***"But if you do evil, be afraid; for he [the ruler] does not bear the sword in vain, for he is God's minister, an avenger to execute wrath on him who practices evil."***
>
> — Romans 13:4

"We know that the law is good if one uses it properly. We also know that the law is made not for the righteous but for lawbreakers and rebels, the ungodly and sinful, the unholy and irreligious, for those who kill their fathers or mothers, for murderers, for the sexually immoral, for those practicing homosexuality, for slave traders and liars and perjurers, and for whatever else is contrary to the sound doctrine."

— 1 Timothy 1:8-10

So God established civil government to regulate the bad guys, not the good guys — it was to reward the righteous and punish the wicked. Too often today, this is reversed, with laws being made to regulate good citizens and too many punishments being inflicted on the righteous rather than on the wicked.

Question #2: Isn't the Constitution our founding document? Then why does it matter what principles are in the Declaration of Independence?

The Founding Fathers actually considered the Declaration to be our founding document, and until recently, Americans held the same view. In fact, even the Constitution dates itself back to the Declaration, and every federal law enacted under the Constitution and signed by any president from George Washington until the present dates itself to the Declaration, not the Constitution.

The Declaration is like a corporation's Articles of Incorporation: it explains the fundamental reasons why the entity exists and the values on which it will operate. The Constitution is like its By-laws: it explains how things will run under the purpose and values set forth in the Articles of Incorporation (i.e., the Declaration).

Significantly, territories become states in the United States through what is called an Enabling Act, which sets forth the requirements for the admission of that territory as a state into the United States. Those enabling acts require that a new state must govern itself according to both the Declaration and the Constitution.

*"Done in Convention by the Unanimous Consent of the States present the Seventeenth Day of September in the Year of our Lord one thousand seven hundred and Eighty seven **and of the Independence of the United States of America the Twelfth** In Witness whereof We have hereunto subscribed our names."*
— Article VII of the Constitution (emphasis added)

2 SESSION

STUDY GUIDE

Furthermore, the Constitution cannot be fully understood or correctly applied without a thorough knowledge of the Declaration, for many of the Constitution's clauses are the direct product of specific grievances enumerated in the Declaration (e.g. Article I, Section 5, Paragraph 4 of the Constitution is the redress of Grievance 4 in the Declaration; Article I, Section 4, Paragraphs 1 and 2 are the redress of Grievances 5 and 6; Article I, Section 8, Paragraph 4 is the corollary for Grievance 7: Article I, Section 8, Paragraph 9 corresponds to Grievance 8; and so forth). The intent of many constitutional clauses cannot be fully grasped or correctly applied unless their corresponding grievance in the Declaration is also consulted and understood.

The Declaration of Independence is indeed our founding document, and it is not to be separated from the Constitution. It is the Declaration that sets forth the five fundamental principles of American government that were later embodied in the Constitution — and four of those five principles that produced American Exceptionalism center directly on God.

Question #3: Many modern academics assert that the Constitution is a Godless document. So how can you claim that our nation was founded on Godly principles?

1. There are 250 or so Founding Fathers, but when today's writers talk about the Founders, they usually only highlight half-a-dozen of them; and the half-dozen they select are usually the least religious of the much larger group. They therefore make an inaccurate portrayal. In reality, the framers of the Constitution were not a group of Godless men. To the contrary, many were theologians, and many more were actively involved in Christian ministry.

2. In an attempt to identify where our Founding Fathers found the unique ideas they incorporated into American government, political scientists embarked on an ambitious project to analyze some 15,000 writings from the Founding Era (1760-1805) with the goal of isolating and identifying the sources referenced in each work. If the source of the

references could be determined, then the origin of the Founders' ideas could be known. The researchers identified 3,154 direct quotations and then documented the source for each. They found that the single most-cited authority was the Bible: thirty-four percent of the documented quotations were taken from the Scriptures — a percentage almost four times higher than the second most-cited source.

3. Many clauses in the Constitution reflect clear Biblical precepts.

   - Article III, Section III, ¶ 2 — Ezekiel 18:20
   - Article III, Section III, ¶ 1 — Deuteronomy 17:6
   - Separation of powers — according to John Adams and others, this feature of our Constitution was derived from the teaching in Jeremiah 17:9
   - Article IV, Section IV — Exodus 18:21

4. Many Framers openly acknowledged that God was responsible for the finished work.

   For my own part, I sincerely esteem it a system which without the finger of God never could have been suggested and agreed upon by such a diversity of interests.

   — Alexander Hamilton, signer of the Constitution

   It is impossible for the man of pious reflection not to perceive in it a finger of that Almighty Hand which has been so frequently and signally extended to our relief in the critical stages of the Revolution.

   — James Madison, signer of the Constitution

   I am as perfectly satisfied that the Union of the States in its form and adoption is as much the work of a Divine Providence as any of the miracles recorded in the Old and New Testament were the effects of a Divine power.

   — Benjamin Rush, signer of the Declaration, ratifier of the Constitution

Others made similar avowals.

2 SESSION

STUDY GUIDE

The claim that the Constitution is a Godless document is a recent revisionist claim and is thoroughly disproved by historical records and original documents.

ADDITIONAL READING/VIEWING/LISTENING

- *Keys to Good Government/Faith, Character & the Constitution* by David Barton
- *God in the Constitution* by David Barton
- *Exceptional!* by David Barton
- *Constitution Alive!* by Rick Green and David Barton
- *The Influence of the Bible in America* by David Barton
- *Documents of Freedom* (available at WallBuilders.com)

DISCUSSION QUESTIONS AFTER WATCHING THE VIDEO

1. In what areas is our government today placing man's opinion above God's fixed moral law?

- Abortion
- Approval of homosexual marriage
- Infringement on churches' and pastors' ability to speak to specific topics
- Taking and regulating private property
- Restrictions and regulations that limit the right of self-defense
- Infringing the rights of religious conscience

2. Is a free society possible aside from the influence of the Bible?

If government refuses to acknowledge that it is an institution ordained by God, and that our inalienable rights come from God and are to be protected rather than regulated by government, then there will be a perpetual infringement by government on the God-given rights of the individual. The result will be a loss of freedom and an increase of tyranny. Secular governments are never limited governments, for they heavily manage every aspect of the lives of their citizens. True political freedom is a result of the application of the Scriptural principles relating to government, society, and culture.

3. What happens when a society rejects the idea of God as Creator?

Romans 1 says that when we stop being God-conscious that our behavior changes for the worse. This is true with both individuals and governments. The belief in a Creator Who loves us and to Whom we are accountable provides a positive restraint on our behavior and incites to sacrificial service rather than selfishness. Apart from God, government becomes a master instead of a servant. Rather than inspiring obedience through love, it coerces obedience by force, becoming steadily more tyrannical, and consistently reduces liberties. A nation can never be happy or free in such a situation, which arises whenever it becomes secular rather than God-conscious. Only living in accordance with the rules established by the Creator can make man truly happy. Those rules provide happiness for the individual and the society, and those rules establish lasting liberty and true prosperity.

SESSION 3

THE ROLE OF GOVERNMENT

"If Congress can do whatever in their discretion can be done by money, and will promote the General Welfare, the government is no longer a limited one, possessing enumerated powers, but an indefinite [unlimited] one..."

— James Madison

3 SESSION

THE ROLE OF GOVERNMENT

INTRODUCTION

Civil Government is one of the three God-ordained institutions. What is its proper role? How should it fit into the life of the average citizen? And what is the proper relationship between Civil Government and other institutions, such as Church and Family?

"Limited" refers not to the size of government but rather its reach — that is, its jurisdictions. The Scripture gives very clear teachings on what government should and should not do — on how it should serve in a limited role; and these jurisdictional principles were incorporated into our Constitution by the Founders. "Limited government" is one of the most important but more ignored and misunderstood principles related to civil government, but whenever the clearly established Biblical lines limiting jurisdictions are honored, society enjoys stability, security, and liberty.

Additionally, all of the rights we enjoy as a result of having a limited government have specific responsibilities accompanying each right. If we ignore these responsibilities, we will lose our rights. This makes it imperative that in every sphere we not only exercise our rights but fulfill our responsibilities.

In today's session, you'll learn:

- The limits God has placed on each institution He ordained
- What the Scripture teaches about limited government
- Why limited government is not possible apart from Scripture
- How this concept has been misapplied by today's government and society
- What the Founders meant by "the laws of nature"

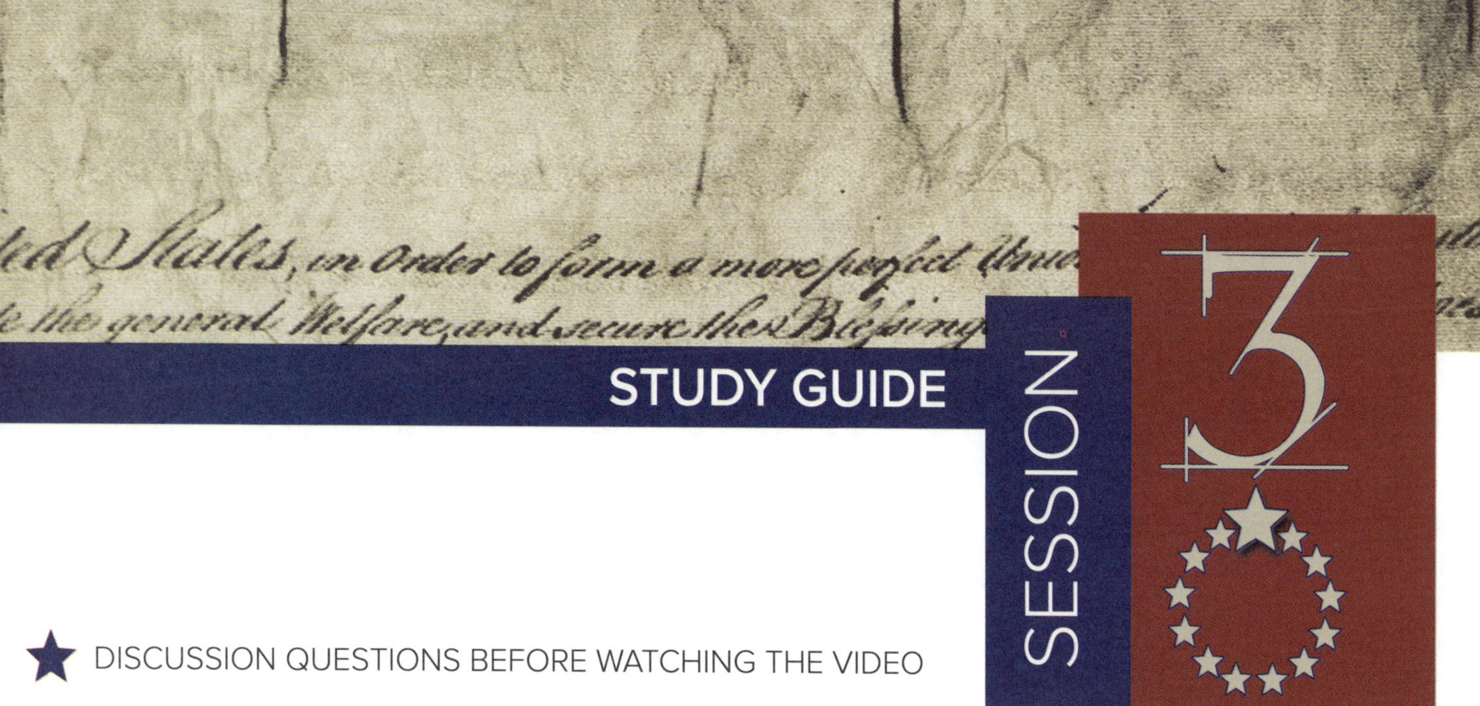

★ DISCUSSION QUESTIONS BEFORE WATCHING THE VIDEO

1. Does the Declaration of Independence have any practical importance to us today?
2. Is America a democracy? What does that mean?
3. Is Civil Government superior to the Church or vice versa?

What is the proper role of government?

The three institutions established by God (in Genesis) are (in this order):

- Family
- Civil Government
- Church

JURISDICTION
the limits or territory within which authority may be exercised.

God, as the Author of all three institutions, gave specific jurisdictions to each, delineating the areas in which each was to function and operate.

For example, the important task of raising up "saints for the work of the ministry" (Ephesians 4:11-12) is designated as the responsibility of the Church, not the Family or Civil Government. And raising children is the responsibility of the Family (Ephesians 6:4), not the Church or Civil Government. Similarly, "bearing the sword" both in the nation's defense as well as in the punishment of the lawless is the responsibility of Civil Government (Romans 13:4), not of the Church or the Family. The Family or the Church may pick up the sword of self-defense but are not to pick up the sword of civil justice. Whenever the Church has done so, it resulted in the types of atrocities that characterized medieval times.

Other jurisdictional lines are also established by God. For example, when God originally established His nation, Israel, he placed Aaron over the religious duties and Moses over the civil ones. Each had separate jurisdictions. Later, when King Uzziah tried to blur the lines by operating

3

SESSION

STUDY GUIDE

as both the king and a priest (2 Chronicles 26 — that is, he attempted to merge both Church and State), God sovereignly intervened and struck Him down. God insisted that jurisdictional lines be observed.

Today, the "separation of church and state" metaphor is routinely abused and misapplied in a way that violates proper jurisdictional lines. Historically, this phrase referred to preserving the lines that God had established between the Church and Civil Government, and it had nothing at all to do with secularizing the public square or confining the influences of religion solely to the Church or the private realm. Under God's design, God was to be intimately involved in all three institutions — He Himself created all three and was to be excluded from none; and He expected each to openly acknowledge Him (which does not violate the Biblical or historical separation of church and state) and to operate within the jurisdictions He had established for that institution.

"Congress shall make no law respecting an establishment of religion, or prohibiting the free exercise thereof; or abridging the freedom of speech, or of the press; or the right of the people peaceably to assemble, and to petition the Government for a redress of grievances."
— The First Amendment to the Constitution

"Also we inform you that it shall not be lawful to impose tax, tribute, or custom on any of the priests, Levites, singers, gatekeepers, Nethinim, or servants of this house of God."
— Ezra 7:24

Today, that understanding has been dramatically reversed. But the actual language of First Amendment to the Constitution still reflects the proper jurisdictional understanding. Its two clauses dealing with religious liberty declare:

- The Establishment Clause — Civil Government cannot establish a national denomination or doctrinal or ecclesiastical hierarchy.
- The Free Exercise Clause — Civil Government cannot hinder the free exercise of religion as practiced according to the dictates of conscience by either individuals or groups, whether done in private or public.

The only limitation in the First Amendment is placed on Civil Government, not the Church, Family, or Individuals. Government thus is to protect, cooperate with, and facilitate the Church, but not control it or its religious beliefs or expressions. But today, the government wrongly prohibits certain religious activities by churches, families, and individuals.

Another manifestation of the original limited power of Civil Government over the Church is demonstrated by the fact that the Church is not to be taxed by Civil Government. The reason behind such a policy was identified by Founding Father John Marshall, Chief Justice of the U. S. Supreme Court, when he declared that "The power to tax is the power to destroy."

Maintaining a truly limited government is possible only when there is a Scriptural understanding of the proper roles and jurisdictions of government. Reflecting this, the U. S. Constitution only allows the federal government to operate in seventeen specific areas and no others. But over recent decades, the federal government has ignored those strictures. A sad lesson consistently demonstrated across the millennia of history is that a secularist government that ignores God-established jurisdictions will never be a limited government.

Question #1: Isn't it good for government to stay out of our churches and families?

Each of the three institutions that God created is separate from the other two, and each is assigned specific exclusive jurisdictions. But there are definitely some areas in which they can cooperate with each other without violating their jurisdictional lines. For example, the Church can help build strong Christian citizens, which benefits Civil Government. And the Family can help build strong spiritual Christians, which helps the Church. And Civil Government can provide an atmosphere that encourages strong families, which benefits both the Family and the Church. It can also provide protection for the expression and operation of religious beliefs and practices of the Family and the Church.

> ***Whatever makes men good Christians, makes them good citizens.***
>
> – Daniel Webster

Significantly, while each of the three God-ordained institutions has limitations placed upon it respecting its specific jurisdictional reaches, Individuals may operate in all three institutions. Thus, an individual can be involved in Civil Government, the Church, and Family at the same time. The restriction is not on the individual but on the powers exercised by each institution, and as long as the Individual recognizes the distinctive limitations placed on each entity, he or she may move freely between them.

3 SESSION

STUDY GUIDE

Question #2: The Founders used the phrase "the laws of nature." Doesn't that language mean that they were really Deists who didn't believe in a personal God or individual faith?

This is a common claim resulting from historical malpractices promulgated by Modernists and Revisionists.

"Modernism" is a contemporary academic approach that severs history from its context and examines historical events and persons as if they occurred and lived today rather than in the past. But in order to accurately portray history, each group or individual must be understood in the context of the beliefs and practices of their own times rather than modern ones. "Revisionism" is a process by which historical fact is ignored, distorted, or misportrayed in order to help facilitate a shift in the general character of a culture.

Because the terms "laws of nature" or "natural law" are rarely used by Christians today, modern educators, academics, and critics therefore routinely conclude that the Founders must have been Deists. But these writers are wrong. The fact we no longer use these terms in today's Christian rhetoric certainly does not mean the terms were deistic. In fact, the direct quotes of the Founding Fathers demonstrate that the terms "natural law" and "the laws of nature" were based firmly on the Scriptures, and these terms were also regularly used throughout countless sermons by even the most evangelical ministers of that day.

(By the way, perhaps the favorite Bible verse of Christians today is John 3:16, which even routinely appears on signs in televised sports events. But search sermons from two centuries ago, even from some of the most theologically-sound Christian pastors, and it is extremely rare that this verse is ever mentioned. The doctrine of God's love and salvation remains unchanged across time, but the popular language to express that doctrine routinely changes across generations. This is certainly true in the difference with much religious rhetoric between the present and the Founding Era.)

For example, examining the "laws of nature," James Wilson, a signer of both the Declaration and the Constitution explained:

> As promulgated by reason and the moral sense, [law] has been called natural; as promulgated by the Holy Scriptures, it has been called revealed law. As addressed to men, it has been denominated the law of nature; as addressed to political societies, it has been denominated the law of nations. But it should always be remembered, that this law, natural or revealed, made for men or for nations, flows from the same Divine source: **it is the law of God**.

Clearly, the "law of nature" is a God-centered term, even though it is largely unfamiliar to this generation. So not only is the term not deistic, but only a small percentage of Founders were deists; the overwhelming majority of them were known as Christians.

For example, among the signers of the Declaration were numbers of strong and outspoken Christians. In fact, 29 of them received their degrees from colleges founded to train ministers; and large numbers of them were directly involved in Christian ministry. Additionally:

- Benjamin Rush started the Sunday School movement and America's first Bible society
- John Hancock, as governor of Massachusetts, called his state to prayer on 22 separate occasions — regularly using evangelical language — and often to days of humiliation, fasting, and prayer as well.
- Rev. Dr. John Witherspoon published the first family Bible
- Charles Thompson produced the famous Thompson's Bible — the first translation of the Greek Septuagint into English (a project that took him 20 years)
- Roger Sherman wrote the doctrinal creed for his denomination and was a treasurer at Yale
- Robert Treat Paine was a military chaplain

3 SESSION

STUDY GUIDE

- Francis Hopkinson was a choir director and music leader who compiled the first purely American hymnbook, setting the entire book of Psalms to music
- Thomas McKean was a judge, and when a defendant was sentenced to death in his courtroom, he stopped the proceedings and delivered a Gospel message and altar call

It is the same story with signers of the Constitution:

- Abraham Baldwin was a theologian and tutor at Yale
- William Samuel Johnson was a theologian who headed Columbia University
- Alexander Hamilton founded the Christian Constitutional Society
- James McHenry started the Maryland Bible Society
- Charles Cotesworth Pinckney and John Langdon were founders of the American Bible Society
- William Livingston was living among the Mohawk Indians as a missionary at the age of 14
- Rufus King was a founder of the New York Common Prayer Book Society

And there are numerous other examples. So contrary to many modern claims, only a small handful of the 250+ Founding Fathers were deists, and the term "laws of nature" was not a deistic term but rather was common rhetoric among the solid Christians and evangelicals of that day.

 ADDITIONAL READING/VIEWING/LISTENING

- *The Principles of Limited Government* by David Barton
- *Original Intent* by David Barton
- *The Role of Pastors and Christians in Civil Government* by David Barton
- *The Founders' Bible* by David Barton

SESSION 3

STUDY GUIDE

 DISCUSSION QUESTIONS AFTER WATCHING THE VIDEO

1. What happens when the Church or Family neglects its responsibilities?

When any institution does not exercise its responsibilities, it creates a vacuum that invites something else to fill the void, which often is government. For example, when the Church began to back away from being the primary source to meet the social welfare needs (a responsibility given it in numerous Scriptures), it left a glaring hole. Those needs had to be met, and the government stepped in. Similarly, when the Family, for whatever reason, began to neglect its responsibility for the education of children, it left a void that the government filled. By neglecting their God-assigned responsibilities, the Church and the Family allowed Civil Government into areas that God had not designated for it. The result is a rapidly expanding government that no longer recognizes jurisdictions but that usurps major responsibilities given to the other two institutions. But regardless of the shortcomings of the other two institutions, it was still wrong for Civil Government to enter those areas, no matter the reason or excuse.

2. What are some ways the Civil Government is encroaching on the jurisdictions of the Church and Family?

- Assuming of the responsibility for education, and then establishing secularism throughout education
- Restricting what pastors can say from the pulpit and even what ministry responsibilities they can undertake in their local communities
- Encouraging licentious sexual behavior in both teens and adults
- Caring for the poor and elderly
- Limiting the ways in which citizens may publicly express their faith
- Assuming the role of defining and regulating marriage

3

SESSION

STUDY GUIDE

3. What can "We the People" do to stop government encroachment?

The first step in stopping this encroachment is to ensure that our families and churches fulfill their God-assigned responsibilities. Next, stand up against improper incursions, just as you would a trespasser who wrongly enters your property. For example, if pastors ignore the unscriptural and unconstitutional pulpit restrictions that the government tries to place on them, this can go a long way to helping restore their lost liberties. Third, many laws need to be changed or repealed, so be active in bringing public awareness and public pressure to bear on elected officials at every level to make those changes. Fourth, recruit and then elect to office those leaders who understand the limited role of Civil Government and what properly belongs to the Family, the Church, and Civil Government.

DEMYSTIFYING THE JUDICIAL SYSTEM

"The first and governing maxim in the interpretation of a statute is to discover the meaning of those who made it."

— James Wilson

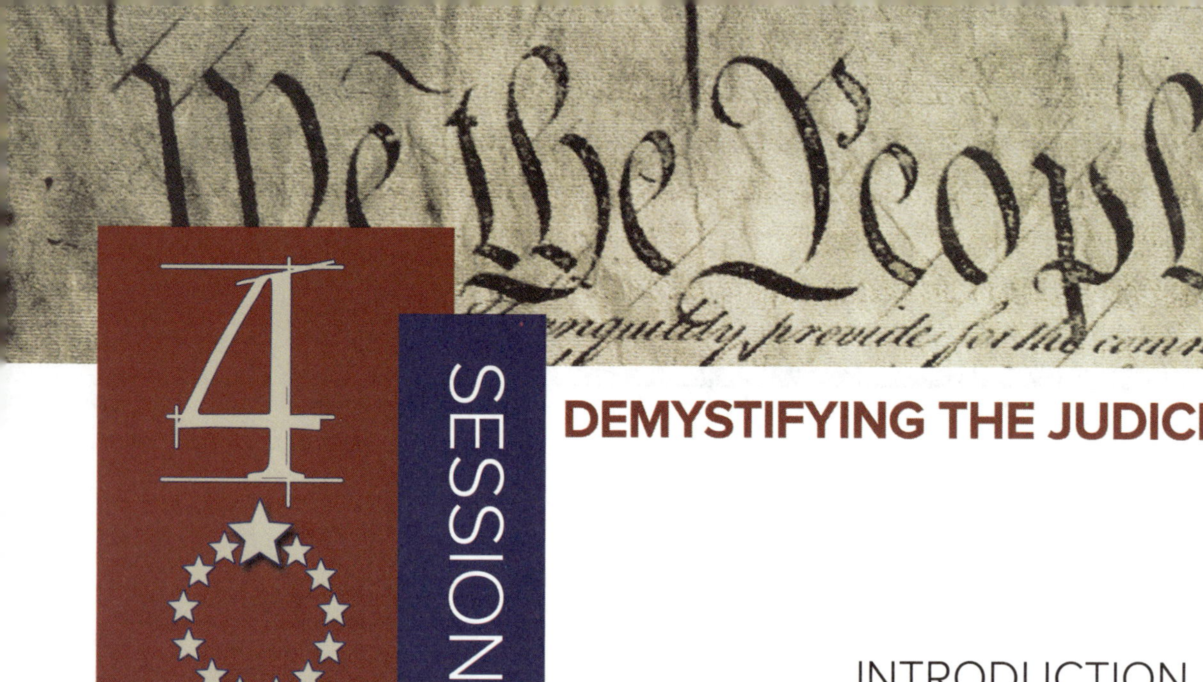

DEMYSTIFYING THE JUDICIAL SYSTEM

INTRODUCTION

What was the purpose of the judicial branch? Are courts and judges to be held accountable for wrong or unconstitutional decisions? If so, how?

The judicial branch is the most misunderstood branch in our system of government today, and it has strayed farthest from the Founders' original design and intent that it be the weakest (by far) of the three branches.

As we now see courts routinely striking down laws passed by Congress, creating their own national policies, ignoring the Founders' original intent for the Constitution, and turning to international law instead of American law, it's more important than ever that we understand what both the Bible and the Constitution say about the judicial branch.

In this session, you'll learn:

- The roots of our American judicial system
- The forgotten role of juries
- The judicial branch's original relationship to the legislative and executive branches
- The constitutional checks and balances for federal judges
- How "We The People" can hold judges accountable

 DISCUSSION QUESTIONS BEFORE WATCHING THE VIDEO

1. What happens when courts are not accountable to the people?
2. How should people hold courts accountable?
3. Should all of the branches be equal with each other? Why?

STUDY GUIDE

SESSION 4

What is the proper role of the Judiciary?

The role of judges is defined by both the Bible and the Constitution. Concerning the former, many verses address the subject of judges and the judiciary. For example:

> *"Take warning, O judges of the earth. Worship the Lord with reverence and rejoice with trembling. Do homage to the Son, that He not become angry and you perish in the way, or His wrath may soon be kindled."*
>
> — Psalms 2:10-12

Judges are also instructed:

> *"Consider what you are doing, for you do not judge for man but for the Lord Who is with you when you render judgment. Now then, let the fear of the Lord be upon you; be very careful what you do."*
>
> — 2 Chronicles 19:6-7

And God also told Isaiah that one way in which Israel (which was then in a period of degeneration) could be restored was by a change in their judges — that if they would return to the type of judges they had in their earlier years, then Jerusalem, their national capital, would again become a center of righteousness. As God explained:

> *"I will restore your judges as at the first, and your counselors [attorneys] as at the beginning; after that you will be called the city of righteousness — a faithful city."*
>
> — Isaiah 1:26

Notice the principle: the righteousness of a land is directly affected by its judges. America clearly demonstrates this, for it has been judges and not legislatures who have imposed on America the vast majority of our unrighteous policies.

4 SESSION

STUDY GUIDE

For example, abortion on demand was not instituted by legislatures but rather by judges who decreed it to be national policy. In fact, the Supreme Court had to strike down anti-abortion laws in forty-six states to achieve its will. Similarly, the movement for same-sex marriage was initiated by judicial decisions demanding that state legislatures set aside four centuries of American laws defining marriage as the union of a man and a woman. Likewise, prohibitions on prayer before school athletic events and graduations, as well as exclusions of the Ten Commandments or other religious acknowledgments in classrooms, are the result not of legislators but of judges. This truly affirms what God said in Isaiah 1:26: the righteousness of a land is directly affected by its judges.

Furthermore, God unequivocally declares that He uses the righteousness of a community as a measure for whether or not to bless it (Proverbs 14:34). Therefore, issues of Biblical righteousness should be the foremost concern when choosing a U. S. President, U. S. Senator, Governor, State Senator, or other official. And because righteousness is directly affected by judges, this means that citizens should elect presidents, governors, and senators only after determining the type of judges they will appoint or confirm. Ezra 7:25 pointedly instructs such leaders to "appoint judges . . . who know the laws of God," and if this directive is not followed, then the righteousness of the nation or a state will be adversely impacted, which will then affect every citizen under its jurisdiction. So be sure to choose leaders who will appoint judges who will perpetuate Biblical standards of righteousness, thus allowing God to bless America, or your state or community.

Understanding the potentially damaging power of judges, the Founding Fathers placed upon them numerous restraints resulting in the establishment of certain key judicial principles with which citizens today are almost uniformly unfamiliar. This has permitted the growth of four modern and completely wrong judicial doctrines, including that:

- Federal judges are appointed for life
- The judiciary is an independent branch of our government
- Only judges can decide what is and is not constitutional
- All three branches of government are equal

Judicial Principle #1

Federal judges are not appointed for life. The Constitution specifically states that federal judges are appointed only for the duration of "good behavior" (Article III, Section 1). Beginning in 1765, Founding Fathers began strenuously objecting against British judges who had lifetime appointments — appointments that thus made them unaccountable. After all, if the judges know they are safely and permanently ensconced in a particular position for the rest of their lives, then what can they be threatened with? The judges became like hereditary lifetime monarchs, knowing that regardless of what they did, they would remain untouched. The Founding Fathers understood this and did not want it, so when they wrote the Constitution, judges were allowed to remain in office only during the duration of "good behavior." Thus, if a judge did not do what he was supposed to, he was removed. The Founders simply did not allow federal judges to have lifetime appointments.

"One thing, however, must not escape our attention....[J]urors possess the power of determining legal questions."
— James Wilson

Judicial Principle #2

The judiciary is not an independent branch. As Thomas Jefferson warned:

> It should be remembered, as an axiom of eternal truth in politics, that whatever power in any government is independent is absolute also.

The Founders did not want any power of government to be independent, which meant it would be absolute over the people. This was especially true with any unelected powers. The Founders intended that every branch be accountable. As affirmed by Founding Fathers such as Samuel Adams, John Hancock, and John Adams in the Constitution of the Commonwealth of Massachusetts:

> All power residing originally in the people and being derived from them, the several magistrates and officers of government vested with authority — whether Legislative, Executive, or Judicial — are their substitutes and agents and are at all times accountable to them.

READ MORE
The Story of Religion in America
by William Warren Sweet

4 SESSION

STUDY GUIDE

A lack of accountability in any arena (even the Church or the Family) encourages tyranny in that realm, and that particularly includes the Judiciary. God does not allow any of us to be unaccountable for our behavior and decisions; neither does the Constitution.

Judicial Principle #3

It is not only judges who can decide what is constitutional. Every official in all three branches of government takes an oath to uphold the Constitution; none of them take an oath to uphold a judge's opinion of the Constitution. To do so would be to say that a judge or court is infallible and can make no mistakes. Such a proposition is ludicrous. As Thomas Jefferson clearly explained to one such misinformed individual in his day:

> You seem... to consider the judges as the ultimate arbiters of all constitutional questions; a very dangerous doctrine indeed, and one which would place us under the despotism of an oligarchy. Our judges are as honest as other men and not more so. They have, with others, the same passions for party, for power, and the privilege of their corps... The Constitution has erected no such single tribunal.

Judicial Principle #4

The three branches are not equal. The Founders deliberately made the legislative branch the most powerful, and the judiciary the weakest, by far. Concerning the legislative branch, James Madison declared: "In republican government, the legislative authority necessarily predominates." And concerning the judicial branch, Alexander Hamilton emphatically affirmed that "the judiciary is beyond comparison the weakest of the three departments of power."

If America is to be regained from the hands of unelected, unaccountable judges, then we must cease believing these four lies that we have been taught in recent years.

(In addition to the Bible passages already mentioned above, many others also address judicial responsibilities and practices. For more of these, see the commentaries in *The Founders' Bible* for 1 Samuel 7, Proverbs 18, Deuteronomy 19, Isaiah 1, and other passages.)

Question #1: How do we hold judges accountable?

Because federal judges are allowed to hold their offices only during "good behavior," then when they act otherwise, they can be removed. Six clauses in the Constitution address the means of removing judges. In fact, more mention is given to this one subject than to any other. The method most often used to remove a judge is that of impeachment. Today, people wrongly believe that the bar for the impeachment of judges is very high — in fact, almost too high to be reached. But the Founders actually placed the bar very low. For example, in America's early years, federal judges were impeached and removed for the following reasons:

- Profanity in the courtroom
- Getting drunk in private life
- Contradicting an act of Congress
- Rudeness to a witness
- Judicial high-handedness

All of this was considered "bad behavior" for judges and therefore qualified them for removal from the bench. So judges are indeed accountable, and Congress can call them to account.

Interestingly, history demonstrates that the more often Congress conducts an impeachment investigation for misbehavior in a judge, the less often they have to actually remove a judge. Clearly, when judges know they are accountable and can be called on the carpet, that knowledge causes them to self-restrain improper behavior, thus limiting judicial activism.

Question #2: Did juries play a more important role in the judicial process of previous generations?

When America separated from Great Britain, the Founders specifically enshrined both the rights and the important role of juries in both the federal and state constitutions. From the beginning, American juries had a two-fold responsibility: (1) examine the facts in a particular case, and (2) judge the law at the center of the controversy. The jury considered both of these areas because it was understood that if a law was tyrannical, then enforcing it would prevent justice rather than secure it. So juries examined both the law behind the case and the facts in the case.

4 SESSION

STUDY GUIDE

> "[T]here is not a syllable in the [Constitution] which directly empowers the national courts to construe the laws according to the spirit of the Constitution..."
> — *The Federalist Papers*, No. 81 by Alexander Hamilton

To illustrate how this two-pronged duty worked, consider what would have occurred if Daniel in the Bible had been a defendant in early American courts. In Daniel's case, a law had been passed declaring that prayers could be offered to no one but King Nebuchadnezzar. Daniel prayed to the one true God and broke the law. He was arrested, prosecuted, convicted, and punished (Daniel 6:7-16).

But if that case had been brought before an early American jury, Daniel would have been immediately acquitted. The jury would have judged the law under which he was being tried as unjust and despotic — that the law violated Daniel's inalienable and constitutional right to pray to his God according to the dictates of conscience. So even if the judge had told the jury that Daniel had definitely violated a clearly written federal law and that the jury must therefore return a verdict of "guilty," the judge's instructions would have been ignored. The jury was a check and balance on the judge to ensure that justice was done.

But in the years leading up to the 20th century, a dramatic shift occurred, with these traditional "courts of justice" devolving into "courts of law." Upholding the law replaced the pursuit of justice. The impetus for this change was a series of jury decisions against megacorporations and monopolies of that day, after which several powerful legal groups began lobbying Congress and the Supreme Court to limit the power of juries.

In 1895, the Court ruled that juries would no longer consider the law in a case but only the facts — that is, no longer would the jury serve as a check against the tyranny of a bad law; instead, they would just be asked to decide whether or not an individual had violated a law, even if that law was unjust. In that same period, Congress passed a law birthing the federal courts of appeals systems.

There had previously been no need for such a system, for juries had always been the final word. But in the new federal court of appeals system, judges began to tell each other (and the judges below them) what the real meaning of the law was. Judges had thus taken control of the law and become its sole interpreters. Juries were still involved, but now the judges controlled the juries. And juries were no longer to be privy to all the facts and evidence in a case, but they would receive only the information that judges allowed them to know. The judge replaced the jury as the most powerful force in the courtroom.

Consequently, had Daniel been tried by a 20th century court of law, he would definitely have been convicted. The judge would have told the jury that the law was clear that Daniel could not pray in the way he did — that Daniel had clearly violated the law and that he must therefore be convicted. Nothing was now more important than following the law as interpreted by judges. In fact, if a jury tried to exercise its traditional historic role of considering not just the facts but also the law, then judges were told to declare a mistrial or overturn the jury verdict.

In the latter part of the 20th century, yet another devolution occurred, this time moving downward from "courts of laws" to nothing more than just "courts." According to current legal definitions, a court is now merely a locale or a body to settle disputes. Recall the progression: securing justice was the original objective of courts; then it shifted to upholding the law; but now it has become merely settling disputes — i.e., ending arguments. Hence, modern courts have shown an eagerness to strike down laws that stand in the way of settling a dispute, preferring instead to impose their own judicially-crafted policy that they believe best ends the disagreement. Under this arrangement, the people's role in the judicial system is the smallest it has ever been in the history of the republic, and justice has been the casualty.

We must regain the knowledge of how important juries actually are in our governmental process, and as citizens, we should never avoid jury duty, for it is the opportunity to ensure that justice prevails. Notice how strongly the Founding Fathers stressed this feature of our government:

> ***The trial by jury is the democratic branch of the judiciary power — more necessary than representative in the legislature... [A] government where there is no trial by jury has an unlimited command over every man who has anything to lose.***
>
> – John Francis Mercer, framer of the U. S. Constitution

4

SESSION

STUDY GUIDE

> ***The jury trial, especially politically considered, is by far the most important feature in the judicial department in a free country... [B]y holding the jury's right to return a general verdict in all cases sacred, we secure to the people at large their just and rightful control in the judicial department.***
>
> — Richard Henry Lee, signer of the Declaration, a framer of the Bill of Rights

> ***The great object of a trial by jury... is to guard against a spirit of oppression and tyranny on the part of rulers... So long, indeed, as this palladium [safeguard] remains sacred and inviolable, the liberties of a free government cannot wholly fall.***
>
> — Justice Joseph Story, "Father of American Jurisprudence"

> ***Trial by jury [is] the best of all safeguards for the person, the property, and fame of every individual.***
>
> — Thomas Jefferson

Justice is important. It is a Biblical concept. And since so many components of traditional justice are Biblically derived, as America has become increasingly secular over the past century, the pursuit of justice has diminished. Americans need to regain the knowledge and understanding of Biblical provisions for justice in the courts. They should also seek and accept every opportunity to serve on a jury, for Biblical-minded citizens serving in courtrooms can help restore justice.

> ***One thing, however, must not escape our attention....[J]urors possess the power of determining legal questions.***
>
> — James Wilson

Incidentally, the *Geneva Bible* and *Foxe's Book of Martyrs* were extremely influential in the early establishment of our American judicial system.

- The *Geneva Bible* contained the Reformers' commentary on the corrupt practices of their age, pointing out where the culture had departed from Biblical teaching, including specifics of the flawed European judicial system
- *Foxe's Book of Martyrs* showed those who had been killed, or martyred, for their Christian faith (primarily through bad judicial process) beginning with Jesus

The Due Process protections that were placed in the U. S. Constitution with the Fourth through the Eighth Amendments in the Bill of Rights were largely due to the influence of these two books in early America.

Question #3: Shouldn't our judges be neutral with no political agenda?

It is the duty of judges to interpret the laws when there are differing legal opinions as to what a law means, but it is not their duty to make public policy through judicially-enacted decrees. The national political debates and the controversial issues raging in a nation should have no influence on any decision the judiciary makes. They are to ensure that the law is applied justly, not determine whether or not it comports with their view of what social policy should or should not be.

Whenever a court overrules a congressional policy that was based on a reasonable reading of constitutional language, it has wrongly invaded the public policy realm, usurped its constitutional role, and wrongly become a political body. The judiciary is not to shape politics or political public policy debates. Certainly, judges do have political opinions; everyone does. But a judge is not to seek to make his personal opinion into public policy through his judicial decisions — which is exactly what too many judges today regularly do.

 ADDITIONAL READING/VIEWING/LISTENING

- *Five Judicial Myths* by David Barton
- *Restraining Judicial Activism* by David Barton
- *The Founders' Bible* by David Barton
- *Federal Practice and Procedure,* Vol. 30,, Sections 6342-6343, to learn about the influence of the *Geneva Bible* and *Fox's Book of Martyrs* on Due Process in American courts
- *1599 Geneva Bible — Patriot's Edition* (GenevaBible.com)

4 SESSION

STUDY GUIDE

DISCUSSION QUESTIONS AFTER WATCHING THE VIDEO

1. How can "we the people" hold our judges accountable?

- Learn the proper role of judges according to the Bible
- Learn what the Constitution and the Founders said about a limited judiciary
- Educate ourselves to recognize the modern judicial myths
- Share that knowledge with others
- Educate our elected officials on both the responsibility and the process of holding the judicial branch accountable
- Elect legislators who understand the constitutional impeachment of judges
- Contact legislators to urge impeachment investigations as necessary
- Get on juries and stand for justice in all decisions

2. Why did the Founders make the Legislative Branch the most powerful, and why did they fear a strong, independent judiciary?

The legislative branch was designed to predominate over the other two because it is the closest to the people and therefore the body most accountable to them by virtue of its frequent elections. An independent judiciary meant an unaccountable judiciary, and both history and the Bible repeatedly demonstrate that any unaccountable entity tends to accrue unlimited power, abuse that power, and become increasingly tyrannical. The people then have diminishing recourse concerning decisions that encroach on or remove their inalienable rights, including those of life, liberty, property, and so forth.

3. In the numerous Bible verses addressing the subject of judges and the judiciary, which principles have direct relevance today?

Psalms 2:10-12 warns judges to honor God and fear Him, lest we all incur His displeasure, and 2 Chronicles 19:6-7 reminds judges that they are to render the same decision that God would render in each case. But today we have far too few judges who are genuinely God-fearing. They have become like the unjust judge of Luke 18 who fears neither God nor man. Isaiah 1:26 reminds us that our public righteousness is based on what judges do, and Ezra 7:25 says that we are to elect leaders who will appoint judges who will rule in the fear of God. So before we select anyone for office, whether mayor, governor, or president, we should inquire and know what they will do with judges and then cast our vote accordingly. We can eventually solve our current judicial problems if we will return to using the Bible and the Constitution as our guide when electing officials at every level of government.

AMERICA'S LOST HEROES: AFRICAN AMERICAN PATRIOTS

"[I]t will be seen that the various conflicts by sea and land which have challenged the energies of the United States have been signalized by the devotion and bravery of colored Americans.... They have ever proved loyal, and ready to worship or die if need be, at Freedom's shrine. The amor patriæ [love of country] has always burned vividly on the altar of their hearts. They love their native land."

— William C. Nell, 1855
first Black American to hold a position in the federal government

AMERICA'S LOST HEROES: AFRICAN AMERICAN PATRIOTS

INTRODUCTION

Too often today, the Founding Fathers are presented as a collective group of slaveholders and racists, with the Revolution being irrelevant to black Americans. But nothing could be farther from the truth.

While slavery was a harsh reality in some of the 13 colonies, a number of the colonies were steadfast in their opposition to slavery, and black Americans made valuable contributions to many colonies in particular and to the nation in general. Some of the Founding Fathers did own slaves, but many more did not, and the strong majority were anti-slavery.

Today's history books regularly ignore the black patriots of the American Revolution, who often played prominent roles in key battles of the war. The true story of the American Revolution is a story of a struggle for freedom, fought by both white and black Americans, seeking liberty for all.

In today's session, you'll learn about:

- How British rule limited black freedom
- Black Americans elected to political office in the Revolutionary era
- Some of the black patriots who fought in the Revolutionary War
- Many of the abolitionist Founding Fathers
- The American Revolution as the heritage of both black and white Americans

DISCUSSION QUESTIONS BEFORE WATCHING THE VIDEO

1. Why do revisionist historians omit the role of black Americans in the Revolution?
2. What difference does it make whether the Founding Fathers were or were not generally a collective group of slaveholding racists?
3. How would it affect today's society if the uplifting role of blacks in the Revolutionary and Founding Eras was taught?

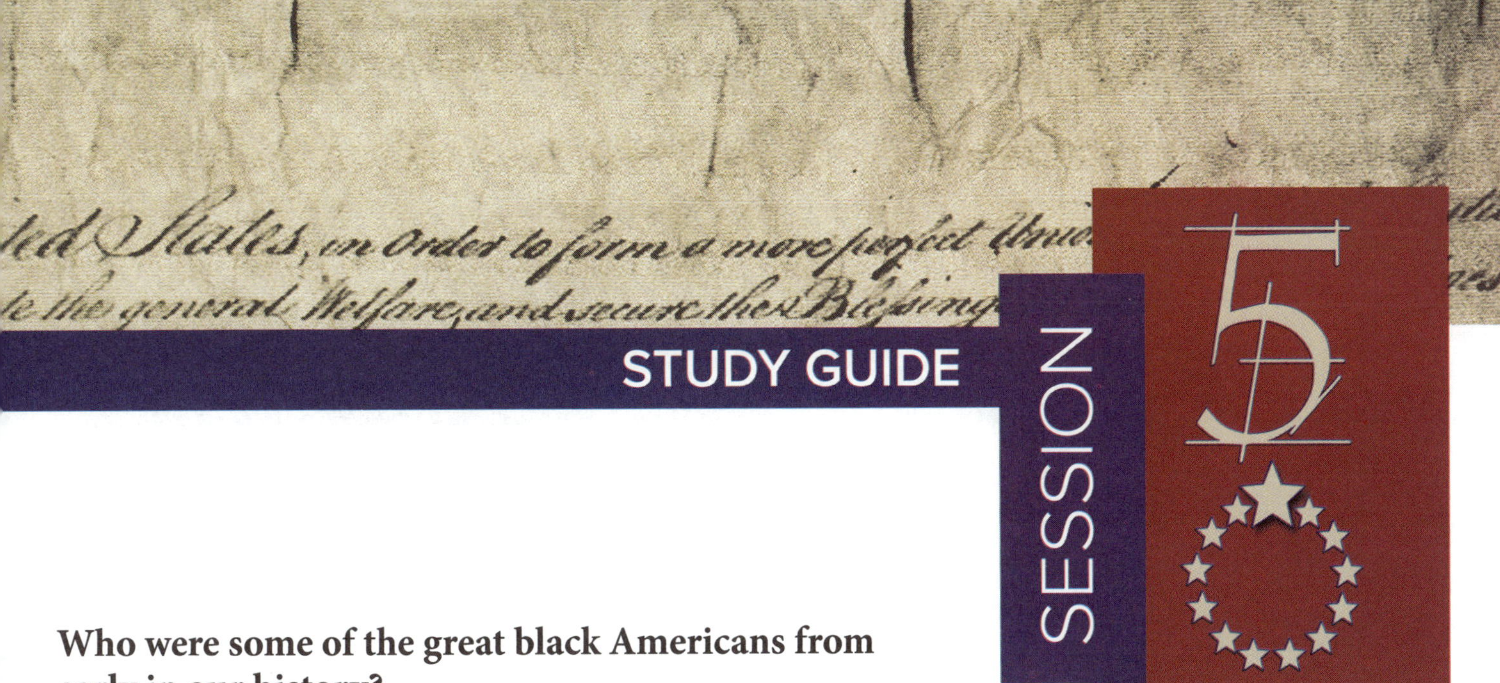

Who were some of the great black Americans from early in our history?

Wentworth Cheswell — the first black American elected to office in America (in 1768 in New Hampshire). He was a church leader, and for 49 years was re-elected to eight different political positions. He is also known as the historian of New Hampshire.

Benjamin Banneker — black self-taught mathematician and scientist, wrote an almanac in the 1790's. James McHenry, a signer of the Constitution, funded the almanac's printing, and Thomas Jefferson sent it to anti-slavery leaders in France to illustrate the great achievements by blacks in America.

Thomas Hercules — elected to office in Pennsylvania in 1793 by a majority of white voters in a white district.

Black Colonial Voting — There was never a time when blacks could not vote in states such as Massachusetts. And in Baltimore, more blacks than whites voted to ratify the U. S. Constitution.

William C. Nell — the first black American to hold a position in the federal government and an historian chronicling the involvement of black patriots in the wars of 1776 and 1812.

Robert Smalls — first black captain of a naval ship in the Civil War, was elected to Congress after the War, and became a military general.

Rev. Hiram Rhodes Revels — the first black U. S. Senator: a preacher and missionary; raised two regiments of black soldiers to serve in the Civil War.

Joseph Hayne Rainey — the first black elected to the U. S. House of Representatives and the first black to preside over the House.

These are just a few examples of the many great black patriots, scientists, and leaders from early American history, demonstrating that blacks have indeed shared in and helped shape the American Dream from the beginning, even during the time when slavery remained strong in some areas of the country.

5 SESSION

STUDY GUIDE

Question #1: The Founding Fathers were racist slaveholders; why should I be proud of them?

Today, it has become a sad practice for too many historical writers to present the exception as the rule. For example, if you show someone a picture of the signers of the Declaration and ask them to name which of the signers owned slaves, they can usually identify no more than one or two. Yet on the basis of that one or two, they too often accept what they have been told — that all the Founders were slaveholders. The typical American can identify none of the anti-slavery Founders.

As an example of what is not reported, in 1773, several American Colonies, such as Rhode Island, Connecticut, and Pennsylvania, began passing anti-slavery laws. But the following year, 1774, King George III vetoed all of those laws. The British position was simple: Great Britain had slavery; as long as America remained a British Colony, she, too, would have slavery. But so firmly did American Founders such as Benjamin Rush and Benjamin Franklin (soon to become signers of the Declaration) disagree, that in 1774 they founded America's first abolition society as a reaction against the King's decision to strike down America's anti-slavery laws.

READ MORE
The History of Slavery and the Slave Trade
by W. O. Blake, 1860

Benjamin Rush went on to head the national abolition movement and helped form the first black denomination in America (the African Methodist Episcopal church). And Benjamin Franklin joined with Francis Hopkinson (another signer of the Declaration) to found a chain of schools to teach academics, Christianity, and the Bible to black Americas — a position contrary to British practice.

"That men should pray and fight for their own freedom and yet keep others in slavery is certainly acting a very inconsistent, as well as unjust and perhaps impious, part."
— John Jay, President of Congress, author of *The Federalist Papers*

Then in 1776, when the Declaration of Independence was written, two of the Founders' grievances in the original draft denounced the king's interference with their anti-slavery laws.

Following America's separation from Great Britain in 1776, Declaration signer Stephen Hopkins, governor of Rhode Island, became the first governor to sign an anti-slavery law, and Massachusetts, Connecticut, Vermont, and other states began passing anti-slavery laws.

Declaration signer James Wilson started the first organized legal training in America, and in his law book for students, he condemned slavery as a violation of both God's law and natural law.

Declaration signer John Witherspoon, president of Princeton, trained both black and white students.

There are many other examples. These anti-slavery Founders are virtually unmentioned today, and the few slave-holding racist Founding Fathers are usually the only ones that most Americans are told about.

Question #2: We always hear about George Washington and other white heroes of the American Revolution. But didn't black Americans also fight for independence?

Absolutely yes — and in large numbers. Some of the famous black patriots during the American Revolution include:

Prince Whipple — slave of William Whipple, signer of the Declaration from New Hampshire. Prince told his master that he could fight better if he were fighting for his own freedom. William agreed and freed him. (By the way, like William Whipple, several American Founders owned slaves as British citizens but freed slaves after becoming American citizens.)

Peter Salem — hero of the battle of Bunker Hill; received numerous military commendations for his heroism; saved scores of American lives; a monument was built to him.

Lemuel Haynes — served in the American Revolution as one of the early Minutemen; after the Revolution, he became a pastor and church-planter, frequently pastoring both black churches and white churches; in his churches he preached sermons on George Washington's birthday about his former Commander-in-Chief; he became the first black American to receive a Master's degree.

Prince Sisson — A key part of a commando unit (like an early Seal Team member or Special Forces soldier) responsible for infiltrating British lines and kidnapping a British general right out of the middle of his camp in one of the more heroic actions of the War.

READ MORE
The Biography of the Signers of the Declaration of Independence, John Sanderson, 1824 (available online at Books.Google.com)

STUDY GUIDE

Prince Estabrook — one of the legendary Minutemen at the Battle of Lexington, he was wounded but recovered and served in other battles in the Revolution.

Jordan Freeman— for his extreme heroism and the courageous sacrifice of his life at Fort Griswold in the Battle of Groton Heights, a monument has been erected to him.

James Armistead — a good friend of General Marquis de Lafayette (and shown standing with the general in a famous painting of the American Revolution), James was the first double spy in American history, feeding important British intelligence back to Generals Lafayette and George Washington, thus helping them win the Battle of Yorktown to end the American Revolution.

And there are numerous others.

Question #3: Did black Americans fight on both sides of the Revolutionary War?

Yes. For example, **John Marrant**, a black American from New York and then South Carolina, fought on the British side. He was a young black musical prodigy who became a Christian and was called to preach as a teenager after hearing George Whitefield preach. But when the Revolution broke out several years later, he was impressed — that is, forcibly made to serve — by the British in the Royal Navy. (Before the Revolution, he had become the first Black American successfully to evangelize Native Americans, working among the Cherokee peoples while still only a teenager.) So there were black Americans fighting on both sides, and sometimes not voluntarily.

 ADDITIONAL READING/VIEWING/LISTENING

- *Services of Colored Americans in the Wars of 1776 and 1812* by William C. Nell (1852)
- *Setting the Record Straight: American History in Black & White* by David Barton
- *The Jefferson Lies* by David Barton

SESSION 5

STUDY GUIDE

 DISCUSSION QUESTIONS AFTER WATCHING THE VIDEO

1. Does focusing solely on the slave-holding and racist side of Revolutionary society help or hurt the anti-racism cause?

To ignore the realities of the many patriotic black Americans (as well as the many whites who labored with and for them in the fight to achieve liberty for all) fuels a negative and hostile climate. Sadly, the tremendous contributions of these black and white heroes are unknown or ignored today, and Americans are wrongly taught that blacks didn't contribute to our country until the 1960's. This engenders anger and frustration rather than optimism and hope, causing those offended to see America solely in a negative light, always expecting the worse and routinely attacking or dismissing the country out of hand, including the many good things about it.

2. Were the Founding Fathers hypocritical about freedom?

A large majority of the Founding Fathers were anti-slavery. Because they lived in a time when slavery was a centuries-old practice inherited from Great Britain, many in those days had not thought much about the subject prior to the Revolution. But once the Revolution began and the issue of freedom came to the forefront of their thinking, many of them freed slaves, passed anti-slavery laws, and wrote and advocated for an end to slavery. Even slave-holders like Thomas Jefferson recognized it as a great evil and, unknown to most Americans today, Jefferson became one of the most-outspoken Founders in condemning slavery and in working for the passage of abolition laws, helping lay the groundwork toward eventual national emancipation. Numerous black Americans praised Jefferson's diligent efforts to end slavery. Those among the Founding Fathers who were truly committed to the preservation and extension of slavery were a definite minority.

READ MORE
The Colored Patriots of the American Revolution, William Nell, 1855 (available online at Books.Google.com)

3. Why should black history matter to non-black Americans?

What happened in American history should be of interest to all Americans. For non-black Americans, there are many black American heroes who should be heroes to them simply because they are American heroes. So, too, for black Americans with the whites who worked so closely with and for blacks. Black patriots played a role in founding our country just like white patriots did. It's our history, it's our heritage, and it's incumbent on us to understand and appreciate the sacrifices of all Americans made on our behalf, whether black, white, brown, or any other, so that we all can preserve and pass on to future generations the liberties they won for all of us.

SESSION 6

REMARKABLE YOUNG AMERICANS

"Children should be educated and instructed in the principles of freedom."
— John Adams

"Learning is not attained by chance; it must be sought for with ardor and attended to with diligence."
— Abigail Adams, letter to her son John Quincy Adams

"[S]ystems of education should be adopted and pursued which may not only diffuse a knowledge of the sciences but may implant in the minds of the American youth the principles of virtue and of liberty and inspire them with just and liberal [unselfish] ideas of government and with an inviolable attachment to their own country."
— Noah Webster

REMARKABLE YOUNG AMERICANS

INTRODUCTION

The Founding Fathers achieved many things that seem remarkable to this generation, and many of them were surprisingly young when they made major contributions. What equipped them to take on so many seemingly unsurmountable tasks? Why were the young people of that day generally so much better educated and prepared than we are today? How can we recapture our waning and sometimes even lost educational prowess?

The Founding Fathers were brilliant men, conversant in a wide vocabulary and mastering multiple subjects — deep, profound thinkers with a strikingly insightful and analytic mental acumen. But this was not unusual for Americans in the Founding Era.

The educational system and cultural expectations of that day combined to produce amazing results in their youth. What people today often accomplish only after several higher-education degrees was often the norm for many teenagers then, for they were raised with the expectation of making great contributions to society. All of this was the result of a forgotten philosophy of education that America embraced for three centuries but has abandoned over the past century.

In today's session, you'll learn:

- The forgotten keys to a successful education
- Why a proper understanding of God is central to sound education
- The type of things children were learning in the Founding Era
- How the Founders approached the teenage years
- What Americans in the Founding Era expected of young people

 DISCUSSION QUESTIONS BEFORE WATCHING THE VIDEO

1. Is it damaging to expect a lot from our children?
2. What does the Bible have to say about adolescence?
3. Can we hold on to our government apart from the educational philosophy that our Founders had?

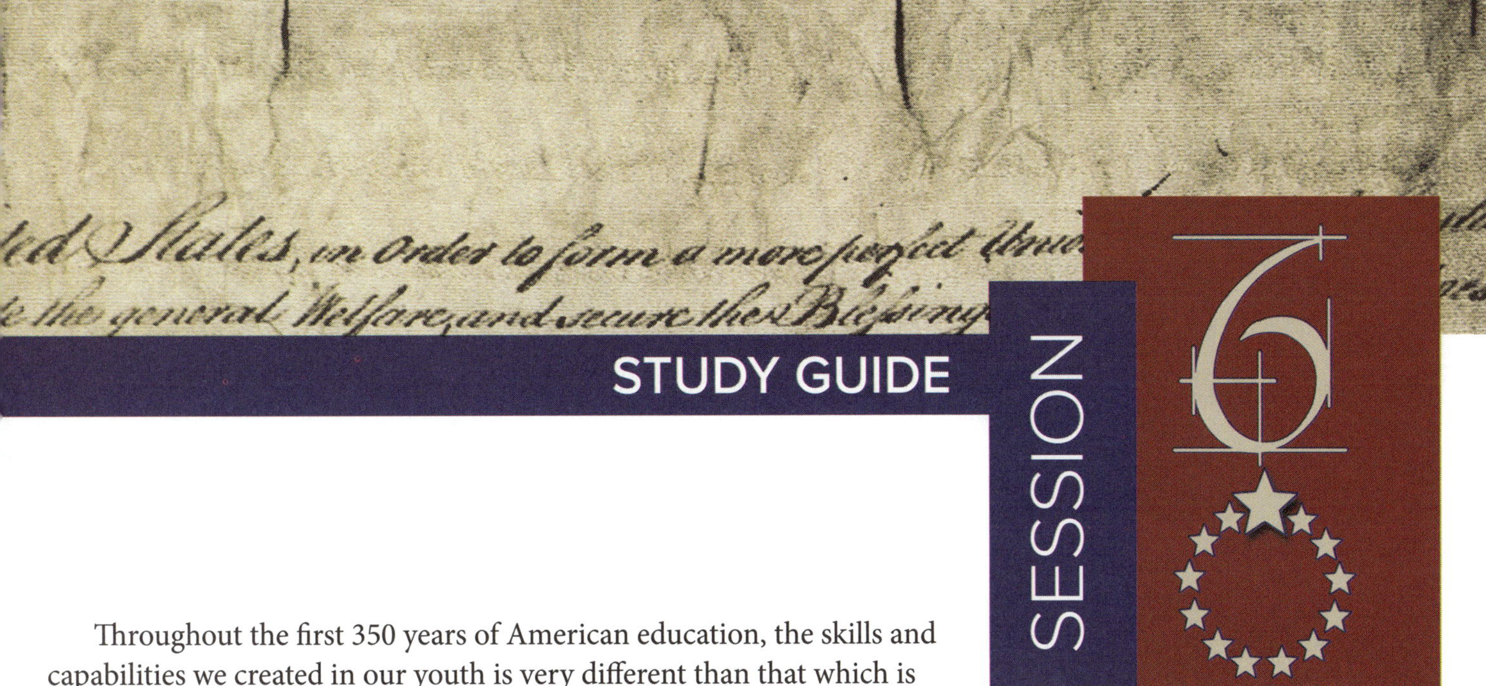

Throughout the first 350 years of American education, the skills and capabilities we created in our youth is very different than that which is generated today.

George Wythe — this signer of the Declaration began a study of the classics when he was 3 years old.

Benjamin Rush — this signer, considered the greatest physician in American history, was 14 when he graduated from Princeton.

William Livingston — when this signer of the U. S. Constitution was 14, he was living among the Mohawk Indians in missionary work.

John Witherspoon — this signer of the Declaration was 4 years old when he finished reading the Bible from cover to cover for the first time.

Thomas Jefferson — this signer of the Declaration began the study of Latin, Greek, and French at the age of 9 and at the age of 16, he entered William & Mary College. (It was common for American youth to enter college between the ages of 13 and 16, and the entrance exam to the major universities of that day required demonstrating a fluency in Latin, Greek, and English.)

John Trumbull — this poet of the American Revolution and Connecticut Supreme Court justice was 4 years old when he read the Bible from cover to cover for the first time; by age 6, he could surpass his minister in translating Greek into English.

Phillis Wheatley — brought to America from Senegal as 6 year-old slave who knew no English. On her arrival in America, she entered studies in English, Latin, history, geography, and the Bible. By the age of 9 she had so mastered English that she was writing poetry; by age 12, her poetry was being published. Her work was highly sought after, including by George Washington, who had her read poetry to his officers during the American Revolution. She was the first black poetess in American history.

"Candidates for admission into Harvard College shall be examined by the president, professors and tutors. No one shall be admitted unless he be thoroughly acquainted with the grammar of the Greek and Latin languages, in the various parts thereof, including Prosody — can properly construe and parse Greek and Latin authors..."
— Harvard College, 1807

SESSION

STUDY GUIDE

John Marrant — when 13 years old in the Founding Era, he became the first Black American successfully to evangelize Native Americans, living among the Cherokees.

James Iredell — when this ratifier of the U. S. Constitution and Justice on the U. S. Supreme Court (placed on the Court by President George Washington) was 17 years old, he was serving as the chief financial officer in his North Carolina region.

READ MORE
John Trumball: Connecticut Wit by Alexander Crowie

John Quincy Adams — when 8 years old, he was drilling with the Massachusetts Minutemen; at 11, he traveled overseas as a secretary for his father, diplomat John Adams; when 14, he received a congressional appointment for diplomatic work in the court of Catherine the Great in Russia; at 15, he was the official secretary for the peace negotiations in France to end the American Revolution.

Andrew Jackson — when 13 years old, this future president was serving in the Continental Army in the American Revolution; when he was 14, he was made a prisoner of war by the British; at 16, he was a schoolteacher.

Maria Mitchell — she was the first woman in America to discover a comet, and she built an observatory. At the age of 11, she was a teaching assistant in astronomy; at 12, she calculated the exact time of a forthcoming eclipse; at 17, she was running an academy, training women in astronomy and science.

"Broncho Charlie" Miller — at 8, he was a bronc buster; at 11, a Pony Express rider, with each of his trips being a ten-day ride at breakneck speed, covering some 1,800 miles between St. Joseph, Missouri, and San Francisco, California, fighting hardships, dangers, storms, Indians, and outlaws along the way.

Louisa May Alcott — this famous literary writer and author of classics such as *Little Women* and *Little Men* was writing poetry at the age of 8; she wrote her first book at age 16 and her first novel at 18, by 19 her works were being published across the country.

John "Little John" Clem — a Civil War hero of the 1863 battle of Chickamauga; for battlefield bravery he was promoted to sergeant by General Rosecrans, and then General Thomas promoted him to lieutenant and placed him on his staff; John was 12 years old.

William "Buffalo Bill" Cody — at 9, he was a cattle driver; at 11, a legendary Indian fighter; at 12, a trapper and woodsman; at 13, a Pony Express rider; at 15, he was riding military dispatches; at 16 he was a guide and scout for the military; he became a Medal of Honor winner.

Annie Oakley — perhaps the best sharpshooter in American history, at 9, she was already earning a living for her family by her skills with a gun.

And there are many additional examples.

Prior to the widespread implementation of the Progressive philosophy of education in the early twentieth century, eighth grade was as high as public education went. After eighth grade a young person was considered an adult and was expected to go to college or enter a career. From the Biblical perspective, children usually became men and women around 13 years old. They did not wallow for years in the non-productivity of adolescence, hanging in limbo somewhere between childhood and maturity. There was no Biblical precedent for adolescence, and it therefore was not a part of early American thinking. The expectations for youth were high, and youth responded accordingly. Sadly, today such expectations are rare — they have become the exception rather than the rule.

READ MORE
Lives of Girls who Became Famous
by Sarah Bolton Knowles

Question #1: Why did schools in America switch from 8 grades of school to 12?

From the founding of the country until the 1920's, the objective of education had been to teach children to think. If students could learn to think, then they had the ability both to acquire and to apply knowledge for the rest of their lives, thus giving them unlimited horizons.

But with the Progressive educational philosophy becoming dominant in the 1920s, major changes occurred: the emphasis shifted from teaching students to think to instead teaching them to learn; the duration of common education increased from eight years to twelve; and compulsory education became the norm. The first change — that of moving from thinking to learning — transferred the focus of education from the student to the teacher. This fundamentally transformed both the purpose and results of education.

6 SESSION

STUDY GUIDE

For generations, students had mastered thinking skills through the use of famous texts such as Watt's *Improvement of the Mind* as well as the broad use of catechisms and forensics. But with the new emphasis on learning, students were instead taught to listen to the teacher and regurgitate back the things they heard from the teacher. The means for measuring student knowledge therefore became fill-in-the-blank, true/false, and multiple choice tests — all means that are designed to have students repeat back whatever the teacher had told them. The teacher thus became the spigot on the faucet of information — the general ceiling on the knowledge students would attain. In short, under Progressive education, rather than teaching students how to fish as had formerly been the case, we simply began to give them fish. Students therefore became dependent rather than independent, thus making indoctrination relatively easy — whatever the teacher believed and knew would become what the students would also believe and know.

Question #2: Was education in the Founding Era only for the elite?

Absolutely not. In fact, the first public education law passed in America (1647) was enacted to ensure that every student in a community could get a good sound education. Public school, or more often called common school education, originated in New England with the early colonies, and then moved southward as other colonies were subsequently added.

Founding Father David Ramsay (a member of the Continental Congress from South Carolina and a surgeon in the American Revolution) praised the New England policy of inculcating both common education and the Gospel to the masses:

> Had I a voice that could be heard from New Hampshire to Georgia, it should be exerted in urging the necessity of disseminating virtue and knowledge among our citizens. On this subject, the policy of the eastern states is well worthy of imitation. The wise people of that extremity of the union never form a new township without making arrangements that secure to its inhabitants the instruction of youth and the public preaching of the Gospel. Hence their children are early taught to know their rights and to respect themselves. They grow up good members of society and staunch defenders of their country's cause.

SESSION 6 STUDY GUIDE

The effectiveness of early American education is illustrated by the practice of a modern law professor. Understanding that when his law students become attorneys they will take an oath to uphold the Constitution, he wants them to fully understand the document to which they will swear allegiance. He therefore requires each student to study *The Federalist Papers*, which is considered the most authoritative original commentary on the Constitution. Those students, enrolled in graduate level legal studies, regularly return to him complaining about the difficulty of reading that book. He nods sympathetically and explains, "I understand your dilemma, for this book was not written for someone at your educational level. This book was written for the common, average upstate New York farmer of 1787. Perhaps someday you'll attain the educational level of those New York farmers!" (*The Federalist Papers* were written as letters to the editors in New York newspapers in 1787 and 1788.)

Clearly, education in the Founding Era definitely was not confined to the so-called elite; it was for everyone, including laborers and workmen such as farmers. That educational system showed itself successful for nearly three centuries. In fact, prior to 1962, America was #1 in the world in literacy, but after the 1962 removal of the Bible and religious principles from schools and the establishment of mandatory secularization by the United States Supreme Court, we fell to #65. But interestingly, the results on standardized achievement tests repeatedly demonstrate that those schools which still incorporate the fear of the Lord in their academic instruction (such as private, home, Christian, and parochial schools) average from 2-4 grade levels higher in academic knowledge than do their counterparts in secular-minded public schools. The Founding Fathers understood that America could not survive without a widely-educated citizenry, and they took diligent efforts to ensure that every American was educated.

> *"A native of America who cannot read and write is as rare an appearance as....a comet or an earthquake."*
> — John Adams

"The fear of the Lord is the beginning of knowledge."

– Proverbs 1:7

Question #3: Isn't it putting too much pressure on young people to raise expectations on what they can do?

Studies have shown that by the time a child is 5 years old, he's gained 50% of all the knowledge he will ever have, and 60% by the age of 6. After that, the learning curve begins to flatten out. So to neglect the first five or six years of a child's life is to lose half (or more) of their most important and productive time for learning. Children don't know what they can or can't do unless told by adults. If we tell them that they likely won't do anything great until they are 25 or so, they will believe that and will act accordingly. If we tell them that they can learn to do much when they are young, then they accept that and (if we will help them and train them) they can attain much more than we imagined. Expectations are key.

Today we have arrived at the point where we convey, either directly or indirectly, that if a student can graduate, get a job, pay taxes, and not get arrested, that he or she will be the perfect citizen. What a low expectation! We also tend to communicate that if a student can graduate from high school, go to college, graduate and get a job, then with perhaps five years of experience they will become mature enough to become contributors to society. How sad that we foster such mediocre expectations for our children.

We need to raise our expectations of what youth can accomplish, and we need to help our children raise their own expectations for themselves. We then need to take time to give them the tools to teach them to think, so that they can feed themselves with objective and useful knowledge for the rest of their lives. Let's raise the bar, and let's equip our youth to accomplish great things!

STUDY GUIDE

SESSION

ADDITIONAL READING/VIEWING/LISTENING

- *Four Centuries of American Education* by David Barton
- *Common Core* by David Barton
- *The Founders' Bible* by David Barton
- *Biographies: Hall of Heroes Series* (available from WallBuilders.com)
- *Noah Webster's Advice to the Young* by Noah Webster (available from WallBuilders.com)
- *Lessons from Nature* (available from WallBuilders.com)

DISCUSSION QUESTIONS AFTER WATCHING THE VIDEO

1. How does today's philosophy of education differ from that of the Founders and previous generations?

Education today is geared towards the group rather than the individual. It is a cookie-cutter, teacher-centered approach where the group memorizes lists and facts given them by the teacher instead of learning to think and feed themselves. In the Founding Era, through the use of forensics and catechisms, children were challenged to think. In fact, textbooks from earlier generations show that students used catechisms on chemistry, astronomy, history, law, geology, and many other subjects. Catechisms help students answer the "Who, What, When, Where, Why, and How?" of a particular topic. They thus gather knowledge for themselves rather than simply repeating whatever others tell them.

2. Is compulsory education a good thing or a bad thing?

It all depends on whether or not the educational system and its philosophy is producing good results or bad. Today, numerous measurements indicate that America's education system is substandard. To compel students to remain in such a system for twelve or more years borders on the criminal, in the broad sense of the word. Competition always brings innovation and higher achievement. If a student can choose a school where he can learn to think, and in which he is able to learn in perhaps 5 years (or whatever) all that he would have learned in twelve years of compulsory education at inferior government schools, then why force them to remain in such a situation? For three centuries, America did not have compulsory education, and academic scores and achievement were markedly higher. It is not that compulsory education itself is the problem but rather that compulsory education was introduced to America as part of enforcing the Progressive educational philosophy — a philosophy that has proven to be a dismal failure.

3. How is our culture of low expectations negatively affecting young people today?

When young people are not encouraged to tackle the thrill and challenges of real-life accomplishments early on, then many times they look elsewhere to fill that vacuum. Too often, this leads to the non-productive or even destructive behavior to themselves and others that is now frequently associated with adolescence. Without a sense of fulfillment that comes from being productive, young people often waste their time and potential in idling and "having fun." As a result, both our country and our youth are missing out on the tremendous personal gratification that comes from the challenges associated with tackling genuine opportunity.

Session 7

CIVIL STEWARDSHIP: DUTY VS. RIGHTS

"I regret that I have but one life to lose for my country."

— Patriot Nathan Hale, last words at his hanging by the British

"Those who expect to reap the blessings of freedom must, like men, undergo the fatigues of supporting it."

— Thomas Paine

CIVIL STEWARDSHIP: DUTY VS. RIGHTS

INTRODUCTION

"Duty" is not a popular concept in our society today, for it requires not only hard work but also a patient perseverance regardless of the outcome. Yet "duty" was a guiding star for our Founding Fathers. They understood that it was a Biblical trait and also believed that every right enshrined in the Declaration and the Constitution had a corresponding citizen duty that accompanied it. They knew that it was impossible to preserve freedom without an associated sense of duty.

Today, as more and more Americans want freedom apart from moral restraint and absent any sense of individual responsibility or personal inconvenience, it is more important than ever that we rediscover the importance of duty, and the Biblical foundation that produces it.

In this session, you'll learn:

- The Biblical basis for duty
- What happens to individuals and societies when duty is neglected
- The key difference between the French and American Revolutions
- The hidden danger of Libertarian thinking
- Why duty has become a neglected character trait today

DISCUSSION QUESTIONS BEFORE WATCHING THE VIDEO

1. Why is duty, both on the part of leaders and individual citizens, so important to a society?
2. Should rights still be protected even when corresponding duties are neglected?
3. Is the public acknowledgement of God a civil right or a civil duty?

STUDY GUIDE

SESSION 7

Throughout the book of Luke, Jesus' disciples witnessed many miraculous displays of His Divine power. They wanted to be able do the same, and had an opportunity to do so when a man approached them seeking assistance for his son; but they were unable to help. Frustrated with their failure, the disciples approached Jesus and understandably asked: "Lord, increase our faith" (Luke 17:5). In reply, Jesus told them an account of farmers and herdsmen, reminding them of all the hard work required in those professions and the lack of appreciation bestowed on such workers. Jesus finished by telling His disciples: "So likewise you, when you have done all those things which you are commanded, say, 'We are unprofitable servants. We have done what was our duty to do.'" Jesus' answer to their request for increased faith was to teach them about doing their duty — to learn to do what was right even when they didn't feel like it, when no one noticed, and especially when no one appreciated it. According to Jesus, learning to do one's duty is key to attaining true spiritual maturity.

Duty was one of the primary traits that characterized early America, and it was a point of emphasis in sermons of pastors, admonitions from statesmen, and instruction in school texts. But the word "duty" means something very different today than what it did at the time of the Founders. In their day, "duty" meant something of binding execution, such as a contractual obligation. But drifting downward from that original meaning, by 1913, it was degraded to "that which one ought to do," and the current definition is now even weaker, being merely a "responsibility." There is a big difference between a responsibility and a binding contractual obligation. Americans must recover the original meaning of duty and must regain the performance of that trait if the nation is to again become healthy.

7 SESSION

STUDY GUIDE

The Founding Fathers firmly held that a duty corresponded to every right — that if we wanted to enjoy our rights, then we had to perform our duties:

> ***The connection between different portions of the same people and between a people and their government is a connection of duties as well as of rights.***
>
> — John Quincy Adams

> ***To each class of rights, a class of duties is correspondent.***
>
> — James Wilson, signer of the Declaration and the Constitution

> ***If it [knowledge] teach man his rights, it also teaches him his duties.***
>
> — Dewitt Clinton, framer of the 12th Amendment to the Constitution

Consider the relationship between rights and duties. For example, an individual has a right to free speech, but he also has the personal responsibility to be truthful with that speech. Similarly, he has a right to keep and bear arms, but he also has a responsibility to use those arms properly and not shed innocent blood. He likewise has a right to freedom of association, but he also has a responsibility to choose associates wisely; and so forth. And while we all have a right to free and good government, we also have a duty to be involved with that government and choose leaders who will keep it free and good. All rights have duties accompanying them.

Significantly, the Founders often identified the performance of our duty as a precursor to receiving spiritual blessings:

> ***The man who is conscientiously doing his duty will ever be protected by that Righteous and All-Powerful Being; and when he has finished his work, he will receive an ample reward.***
>
> — Samuel Adams, signer of the Declaration

> ***All that the best men can do is to persevere in doing their duty… and leave the consequences to Him who made it their duty, being neither elated by success (however great) nor discouraged by disappointment (however frequent and mortifying).***
>
> — John Jay, president of the Continental Congress, original Chief Justice of the U. S. Supreme Court

STUDY GUIDE SESSION 7

The sum of the whole is that the blessing of God is only to be looked for by those who are not wanting in the discharge of their own duty.

— John Witherspoon, signer of the Declaration

Doing one's duty is what God is looking for from us — it is a mark of spiritual maturity. Christians need to regain the concept of duty, and we would do well to adopt the motto that characterized the lifelong efforts of Founding Father John Quincy Adams: "Duty is ours, results are God's."

When rights are separated from duties, then selfishness and individual anarchy are enshrined, and this is especially true when the moral duties associated with freedom are neglected or ignored. Whenever we abandon God's moral standards, and the duty we have to conform to those standards, we invite increasingly coercive government in attempts to restrain the bad behavior that results.

The French Revolution was based on the libertarian idea of freedom without religious morality. The French believed that morality came from education, not religion; the result was a despicable bloodbath. The American Revolution was based on an opposite belief — that religious morality was inseparable from freedom, and the result was one of the most atrocity-free (from the American side) revolutions in the history of the world. America's Founders understood that freedom and limited government were the result of embracing and living by God's moral standards. As George Washington explained:

> "And let us with caution indulge in the supposition that morality can be maintained without religion... Whatever may be conceded to the influence of refined education on minds of peculiar structure, reason and experience both forbid us to expect that national morality can prevail in exclusion of religious principle..."

In order to truly be a useful citizen, you must embrace Biblical morality and be willing to perform the various duties associated with the rights given us both by God and country.

"Men, in a word, must necessarily be controlled, either by a power within them, or by a power without them; either by the Word of God, or by the strong arm of man; either by the Bible, or by the bayonet."
— Robert Winthrop, Speaker of the House, historian

"We have no government armed with power capable of contending with human passions unbridled by morality and religion."
— John Adams

"He is the best friend to American liberty who is the most sincere and active in promoting pure and undefiled religion and who sets himself with the greatest firmness to bear down profanity and immorality of every kind. Whoever is an avowed enemy of God, I scruple not [hesitate not] to call him an enemy of his country."
— John Witherspoon

7 SESSION

STUDY GUIDE

Question #1: Why does it seem that Americans were willing to sacrifice more in earlier generations?

The stronger our Biblical worldview, the more willing we are to set aside our own desires and pleasures, but current polling and surveys show that today, less than 10% of Christians hold a Biblical worldview. Previous generations understood and embraced Biblical teachings, thus denying themselves and doing their duty regardless of the cost. But today, the considerations of convenience and comfort regularly rise above the demands of duty.

Significantly, duty was the quintessential character trait of Jesus. Jesus loved us because it was the right thing to do, and He went to the cross because it was the right thing to do, and He forgave us because it was the right thing to do. It was His duty, and he did it, even though it was unpleasant and painful to do so.

"But remember, that 'none liveth to himself.' Even our old age is not our own property. All its fruits of wisdom and experience belong to the public. 'To do good' is the business of life. 'To enjoy rest' is the happiness of Heaven."
— Benjamin Rush

Duty was also a readily-evident character trait in early America. In fact, many of the Founders personally preferred to remain at home with their families and careers and not be in public life. They also were not thrilled with the prospect of having to defend their liberties at risk of life and limb. But they did both because it was their duty to do so. To have done less would have been to yield to selfishness — to their own preferences and inclinations. The Founders performed their duty even though it cost them greatly. As John Adams affirmed:

> "Posterity! You will never know how much it cost the present generation to preserve your freedom! I hope you will make a good use of it! If you do not, I shall repent it in Heaven that I ever took half the pains to preserve it."

Question #2: A lot of schools today still encourage character traits. But are they the same traits we always taught in America?

In the Founding Era, character traits were largely based on timeless Biblical principles, but today some of the most popular character traits are instead based on ever-changing modern cultural standards and trends.

For example, current traits usually include those of tolerance, non-discrimination, and the importance of not offending others, but as these traits are defined today, they lack a Biblical basis.

Tolerance now means to embrace and to say nothing negative about sexual practices and morals that violate explicit Biblical commands and morality.

Non-discrimination means to welcome into your group anyone, regardless of their beliefs and practices. But on its face, non-discrimination is a ridiculous "character" trait. After all, a wise person discriminates in everything he does — that is, he examines the differences, judges the results, and then makes wise choices based on those measurements. He therefore discriminates between the banks that might hold his money, among the car dealers from whom he might purchase a car, and even the type of food he might consume. So, too, with the type of friends that he chooses (see 1 Corinthians 15:33).

And not offending others now means to avoid saying anything that might make someone else uncomfortable. Yet Jesus' entire ministry repeatedly involved making others, both friends and enemies, uncomfortable. It was not His objective to make others uncomfortable; rather, it was His objective to speak the truth, but that routinely involved confronting the ways in which their lives and thinking did not conform to what God wanted. However, not offending others today often means not telling them the truth — including about their choices and behaviors and what those choices might produce.

Even "hate" has been redefined to be the most loathsome of all possible modern evils — something to be avoided on all occasions. But God Himself practices "hate," for He hates "a false witness who pours out lies, and a person who stirs up conflict in the community" (Proverbs 6:16-19). Indeed, if we are in relationship to God, we are specifically instructed to hate evil — to hate those things that violate God's moral standards (Proverbs 8:13). Strikingly, according to the Bible, there are numerous times when tolerance is a sin and hate is a virtue, but not in today's culture.

7 SESSION

STUDY GUIDE

Some of today's most popular "character traits" taught in schools and across society not only lack a Biblical basis but actually directly oppose unequivocal Biblical teachings. But contrast this with the character traits regularly taught to students in previous generations.

In 1792, Founder Noah Webster ("Schoolmaster to America") wrote a popular school textbook whose character traits included obeying parents, loving God, respecting those in authority, displaying kindness, pursuing justice, paying debts, not stealing, and treating women with respect and dignity. And in 1844, another popular public school text taught the character traits of truth, obedience, industry, honesty, politeness, benevolence, purity, gratefulness, aversion to profanity, respect of parents, and duty to God. Check today's school books and you will find a disturbing absence of most of these earlier Bible-based character traits.

Of the many character traits taught in the Bible, Declaration signer Benjamin Rush identified one as being particularly important:

> "I think I have observed that integrity in the conduct of both the living and the dead takes a stronger hold of the human heart than any other virtue."

The lessons of history (as well as Dr. Rush's own personal experience) had taught him that an individual, whether living or dead, was most often remembered for his integrity (or lack thereof). Dr. Rush provided a concise definition of integrity:

> "By integrity, I mean... veracity [devotion to the truth], fidelity to promises, and a strict coincidence between thoughts, words, and actions."

Integrity is a consistency between what one thinks, says, and does — it is when actions actually match words and motives, and when all are based on truth.

Integrity — the performance of one's word — is a trait readily visible in the signers of the Declaration. To secure their objective for all Americans, the Founders avowed that "we mutually pledge to each other our lives, our fortunes, and our sacred honor," and history demonstrates that the signers of the Declaration did indeed keep their word, and at a high cost.

Of the fifty-six signers, two died at the hands of the British, and seven others died during the war; two were wounded in battle; five were made prisoners of war; seventeen lost their estates or fortunes; five incurred heavy debt by personally financing the war; fourteen lost their families or were separated from them; two lost children; and three lost their wives. There is not a single recorded instance of any of the fifty-six refusing to deliver on his promise or failing to keep his word.

"Lord, who may abide in Your tabernacle? Who may dwell in Your holy hill?...He who swears to his own hurt and does not change..."
Psalm 15:1,4b

Not surprisingly, integrity was readily apparent in the lives of Bible heroes such as Abraham, Job, Daniel, Joseph, Jesus, and so many others. Joseph Story (a "Father of American Jurisprudence") wisely observed:

> "To secure integrity, there must be a lofty sense of duty and a deep responsibility to future times as well as to God."

Integrity requires a deep sense of answerability to God. Recall that before the signers of the Declaration pledged their "lives, fortunes, and sacred honor," they first declared their "firm reliance on the protection of Divine Providence." If there is not a genuine mindfulness of God and of our personal accountability to Him, then there is less awareness of the consequence of not keeping one's word, and therefore less incentive to do so.

READ MORE
Lives of the Signers of the Declaration of Independence
by Benson Lossing, 1848
(available at WallBuilders.com)

Question #3: What duties do I have in the civil arena?

Proverbs 14:34 declares that "Righteousness exalts a nation, but sin is a reproach to any people." Thus, a community is blessed by God on the basis of how well its public policies conform to His general principles. What causes good policies to be enacted? Proverbs 29:2 answers that question, explaining that "when the righteous rule, the people rejoice; when the wicked rule, the people groan." Placing God-fearing people in office is the best means to ensure that policies will be enacted that God can bless; and in America, the only way in which competent God-fearing people will be put into office is if God-fearing citizens elect them. But modern Christians have not done very well in this regard, for up to half of Christians today do not vote — they selfishly refuse to do their duty to God and country.

7 SESSION

STUDY GUIDE

A good Constitution is truly a blessing, but without good leaders it can be absolutely worthless. Consider Israel as example: Did any nation in the history of the world have better laws? Certainly not, for God Himself had written them. Yet how good were those laws under rulers such as Ahab and Jezebel, or Manasseh, Jeroboam, Rehoboam, or other bad leaders? Even though their laws had come from God, these laws were ignored when placed in the hands of unGodly and deficient leaders.

The duties associated with Christian citizenship were an area of heavy emphasis from the pulpit in early America. For example, in 1840, the Rev. Mellish Irving Motte told his parishioners:

> "You... should deposit your vote for office with a religious sense of accountableness like that which makes you so serious when you handle the emblems of the Savior's body and blood."

Wait! Voting was to be considered as sacred as the Sacrament of Communion? Today such a notion would be shouted down as heresy. But based on Biblical teachings, previous generations understood that the same sober-minded sense of individual accountability to God that was to precede Communion was also to precede and accompany citizen voting.

In 1803, the Rev. Mathias Burnet had similarly admonished:

> "[L]ook well to the characters and qualifications of those you elect and raise to office and places of trust... Think not that your interests will be safe in the hands of the weak and ignorant; or faithfully managed by the impious, the dissolute and the immoral. Think not that men who acknowledge not the providence of God nor regard His laws will be uncorrupt in office, firm in defense of the righteous cause against the oppressor, or resolutely oppose the torrent of iniquity... Watch over your liberties and privileges, civil and religious, with a careful eye."

STUDY GUIDE SESSION 7

The Rev. Charles Finney, the renowned revivalist and theologian of the Second Great Awakening, therefore pointedly warned Christians:

> "The Church must take right ground in regard to politics. . . . [T]he time has come that Christians must vote for honest men and take consistent ground in politics or the Lord will curse them. . . . Christians have been exceedingly guilty in this matter. But the time has come when they must act differently. . . . God cannot sustain this free and blessed country which we love and pray for unless the Church will take right ground. Politics are a part of a religion in such a country as this, and Christians must do their duty to the country as a part of their duty to God. It seems sometimes as if the foundations of the nation were becoming rotten, and Christians seem to act as if they thought God did not see what they do in politics. But I tell you, He does see it, and He [God] will bless or curse this nation according to the course they [Christians] take [in politics]."

There are countless additional admonitions from Christian leaders across the pages of American history, and they attest to the solemn reality that the current condition of our country and its government is simply a reflection of the action — or more specifically, the lack thereof — by the God-fearing community.

Where America largely finds itself today is exemplified by the parable in which Jesus described a man who had a good field, growing wheat, but awakened one morning to find the wheat intermingled with weeds. How did it change from good to bad? In Matthew 13:25, Jesus identified the problem: while the good men slept, the enemy came in and planted the weeds. Jesus never faulted the enemy for doing what he did; the problem was that the good men went to sleep. When we go to sleep concerning the nation that God has given us, we fail to do our duty and we open the doors to that which is bad.

7 SESSION

STUDY GUIDE

Our civic duties include:

1. Being an informed citizen — seeking out rather than avoiding information on key issues
2. Being an active citizen — acting on the information we gather
3. Identifying God-fearing leaders for office at every level of government
4. Voting for those leaders
5. Informing other voters about those leaders, even creating local voters guides, if necessary, and distributing that information
6. If there are no good leaders, then recruiting God-fearing candidates for office, or running yourself if need be
7. Contacting your elected leaders, providing them helpful information and asking them to take specific stands
8. Helping God-fearing leaders by doing occasional volunteer work in their offices
9. Contributing to God-fearing candidates and doing occasional volunteer work in their campaigns
10. Using social media, blogs, word of mouth, letters to the editor, or periodic newsletters or emails to educate others about policies and leaders

RECOMMENDED RESOURCES
ChristianVoterGuide.com
and
NationalBlackRobeRegiment.com

ADDITIONAL READING/VIEWING/LISTENING

- *Biblical Principles and the Political Process* by David Barton
- *A Nation Adrift* by Timothy Barton
- *Keys to Good Government/Faith, Character, and the Constitution* by David Barton
- *Religion and Morality: Indispensable Supports* by David Barton

SESSION 7

STUDY GUIDE

 DISCUSSION QUESTIONS AFTER WATCHING THE VIDEO

1. How is French-Revolution-type thinking infiltrating our country?

Any time we make fiscal issues and limited government more important than cultural issues and the acknowledgement of God, we have fallen prey to the type of Libertarian thinking that pervaded France. The Libertarian movement, while purportedly seeking some admirable objectives, reverses Biblical priorities and thus is too often built around the French Enlightenment ideas that separate or dismiss religion and morality from government policies and actions.

2. Why is integrity so important?

Integrity involves both what is done in private and in public. But probably 99 percent of what occurs in government is done in private, so if there is no integrity, the rights of citizens will be sold or traded away without citizen knowledge. Significantly, John Adams identified a politician as someone who would compromise principles for personal gain and a statesman as someone who would not compromise principles, regardless of what it might cost him. What made the difference? According to Adams, a statesman embraced the Biblical reality that he would stand before God and account for his behavior while in office. This awareness served as a restraint on personal misbehavior, for even though we call them "public officials," most of what they officially do actually occurs in private. And because integrity is best secured by the knowledge of accountability to God, then having private integrity is more likely from leaders who are truly God-conscious and God-fearing. (By the way, John Adams made clear that he was not a politician but would remain a statesman, explaining that "The duration of future punishment terrifies me.")

But just as we should expect and demand both private and public integrity from our elected officials, we should also demand it from ourselves. After all, we tolerate in others what we first tolerate in ourselves; if we lack integrity, we won't expect it in others — if we do not keep our word to our spouse, children, employer, neighbor, acquaintance, pastor, or whomever, then we will not really expect our leaders to keep their word either. Go back and review your conversations and see if you made any promises that you have not kept; if so, go secure your integrity and keep your word.

SESSION 8

THE TRUTH OF AMERICAN EXCEPTIONALISM

"Let the American youth never forget that they possess a noble inheritance bought by the toils and sufferings and blood of their ancestors — and [the] capacity (if wisely improved and faithfully guarded) of transmitting to their latest posterity all the substantial blessings of life, the peaceful enjoyment of liberty, property, religion, and independence."

— Joseph Story, United States Supreme Court Justice, "Father of American Jurisprudence"

8 SESSION

THE TRUTH OF AMERICAN EXCEPTIONALISM

INTRODUCTION

Is America exceptional? Is it conceited and nationalistic to think or say so? In Lesson #2, we learned the principles that caused exceptionalism. Now we will cover the reality of this exceptionalism and what it means in modern day-to-day life and living. For centuries, the difference between America's stability and prosperity, and the tyranny, oppression, and chaos experienced by so many other nations has been striking.

The fact that America has been different from the norm isn't by chance or accident. It is the result of implementing certain specific principles. And the exceptional results those principles produce can be experienced by any nation who will adopt those principles and inculcate the values on which they are based.

Interestingly, those principles and the resulting exceptionalism are under direct attack in a way never before experienced in America. In fact, those today who dare to suggest that America is exceptional are regularly and openly attacked, mocked, and derided by leaders throughout politics, media, and especially academia. Yet in spite of the Progressive and Deconstruction Negativists who want to bury the true facts of our nation's founding, the reality is that the principles that made us great as well as the results they produced are boldly written throughout the pages of history for anyone who wants to identify and return to them.

In this session, you'll learn:

- What causes exceptional stability, prosperity, and liberty in a nation
- Why the principles that produced our exceptionalism have been suppressed and hidden from the current generation
- Why focusing on demographic groups rather than individuals is dangerous to the health and longevity of a nation
- Why it's okay to say that our country is exceptional
- How to recover and preserve our exceptionalism

STUDY GUIDE

SESSION

 DISCUSSION QUESTIONS BEFORE WATCHING THE VIDEO

1. Is America truly exceptional, or is such a claim merely (as critics assert) nothing more than nationalistic hyperbole? Why?
2. Why is there so much opposition to acknowledging the reality of the American experience and what it has produced?
3. Has our exceptionalism been greater in the past than it is now?

America truly is exceptional — she definitely is the exception rather than the rule. Consider, for example, the category of national stability.

America has had only one form of government since the U. S. Constitution went into effect in 1789, but France has had fifteen constitutions during the same period: Haiti, twenty-three since 1801; Venezuela, twenty-five since 1811; Brazil, seven since 1822; Ecuador, twenty since 1830; The Philippines, seven since 1899; Russia, four since 1918; Poland, seven since 1919; Nigeria,, nine since 1922; Afghanistan, six since 1923; Iraq, four since 1925; South Africa, five since 1931; Thailand, seventeen since 1932; South Korea, six since 1948; China, four since 1954; Ghana, four since 1957; and so forth. Political instability characterizes nations across Europe, Africa, Asia, South America, and generally the rest of the world — except America. The stability America enjoys truly is uncommon, or exceptional.

Additionally, America is unsurpassed in creativity. We have four percent of the world's population and we should therefore produce four percent of its creativity, but this is certainly not the case. Each year America's meager four percent produces more inventions and patents than the other 96% of the world combined. Our four percent also produces more than half the world's Nobel Prizes in Physics, Chemistry, Medicine, Literature, Peace, and Economic Sciences. And we also produce an amazing 25% of the world's gross domestic product (GDP). None of this is because we have greater natural resources than others, for in so many important categories, many other nations have more natural resources than we do.

The fact that America is the exception and not the rule was already obvious long ago. In 1831, Frenchman Alexis de Tocqueville traversed America and published his findings in Democracy in America, declaring even then that: "The position of the Americans is therefore quite exceptional, and it may be believed that no democratic people will ever be placed in a similar one."

So, American Exceptionalism simply describes the unprecedented freedom, stability, and prosperity that are the result of institutions and policies produced by a unique governing philosophy. But notice the sequence: the fruits that we enjoy in America (such as stability, creativity, and prosperity) are the result of institutions and policies that are produced by a particular philosophy. Obviously, then, identifying the underlying philosophy is the most important part of understanding the reason for American Exceptionalism.

E Pluribus Unim:
"Out of many, one."

As previously noted in Lesson #2, the articulation of that unique philosophy is found in 126 words in the Declaration of Independence that set forth the five principles of American government — principles subsequently encapsulated in the Constitution. And recall that four of those five principles are God-centered. It is therefore interesting to note that the most vocal critics of American Exceptionalism today are generally the secularists in academia and media. It seems that they, more than any other group, oppose the concept of Exceptionalism apparently more for its God-centered causes than its excellent results.

Today, many influences work to undermine American Exceptionalism.

STUDY GUIDE

SESSION 8

1. Poststructuralism and Anti-nationalism.

Dividing a unified nation into groups and subsets.

Poststructuralism and Anti-nationalism focus on division instead of unity — on dividing America into and recognizing Americans by groups rather than as individuals. This is commonly known as "Identify Politics," and it urges a loyalty to something smaller than the nation. Hence, many individuals no longer identify themselves as Americans first but rather as Homosexuals, Feminists, Union Members, Latinos, African-Americans, Seniors, and so forth. In fact, Congress now passes "hate crime" laws determining which subgroups will receive extra protection (such as gays and lesbians) and which will not (such as veterans and seniors). Congress also passes tax laws economically rewarding some subgroups and punishing others. Thus, many laws no longer apply equally to all Americans but differ based on varying groups and identities.

America was long characterized by the Latin phrase on the Great Seal of the United States: *E Pluribus Unum*, meaning "out of many, one." This acknowledged that there was much diversity in America, but that there was a common national culture and unity that transcended all differences. But Anti-nationalism reverses that emphasis to *E Unum Pluribus* — that is, "out of one, many," thus dividing the nation into separate groups and components with no unifying or overarching commonality among them.

2. Deconstructionism and Negativism.

Pointing out and emphasizing the negatives and diminishing or ignoring the positives.

Deconstructionism and Historical Negativism is a steady flow of belittling and demeaning portrayals of Western heroes, beliefs, values, and institutions.

An accurate presentation of history depends on telling the good, the bad, and the ugly about any event, person, or period, but Deconstructionists and Negativists stress the bad and the ugly while

SESSION

STUDY GUIDE

routinely ignoring the good. They can identify every blemish that has appeared on the face of America over the past four centuries but not what has made our country the envy of almost every people in the world — every people, that is, except many modern Americans who can now recite more of what's wrong with America than what's right.

An example of the modern altering of the way that America is now presented to students is illustrated with Alexis de Tocqueville's Democracy in America. That original 1835 work is nearly three inches thick, but today's modern version used in schools is only about ½ inch thick. Significantly, the current edition states that it is "edited for the modern reader." So what does the "modern" reader not need to know that de Tocqueville originally told readers in his day? A comparison of the original with the new version reveals that most of de Tocqueville's observations on the importance of religion, family, morality, and marriage have been removed. Apparently, modern readers don't need to know about America's traditional Biblical values, beliefs, and institutions.

Similarly, in the 1960s, historical writers adopted what is called the economic view of American history, in which they claimed that nearly everything that occurred in American history was principally the result of economic factors. This, of course, ignores significant and powerful historical motivations such as religious freedom, liberty, equality, civil rights, and so forth.

Reflecting this approach, most history books today present the primary cause of the American Revolution as being taxation without representation — an economic cause. But that issue is just 1 of the 27 grievances listed in the Declaration and is actually only Grievance #17 out of the 27. There were numerous other causes listed much higher. Many of the issues ignored today include the:

- 4 grievances in the Declaration dealing with judicial abuses
- 7 grievances dealing with military abuses
- 11 grievances dealing with legislative abuses
- 2 grievances in the original draft that dealt with their desire to abolish slavery

Another example of modern revisionism is seen in a popular textbook that presents the famous words of Founder Patrick Henry as: "Is life so dear, or peace so sweet, as to be purchased at the price of chains and slavery?... I know not what course others may take, but as for me, give me liberty, or give me death!" But notice the ellipsis (the three dots) indicating that some text was removed. What words were taken out? "Forbid it, Almighty God!", thus affirming the deliberate attempt to omit any religious acknowledgment from the current presentation of our history.

"Of all the disposition and habits which lead to political prosperity, religion and morality are indispensable supports. In vain would that man claim the tribute of patriotism who should labor to subvert these great pillars."
— George Washington

But despite today's efforts to deny the obvious, the fact remains that the prosperity, stability, and liberty that we enjoy are derived from a set of specific ideas, and these ideas focus on and were derived from God-centered teachings and the Bible.

Question #1: Given the numerous economic, racial, religious, and political people groups that now exist, how can we not look at history from the viewpoint of groups?

Notice a central teaching of the Bible: Jesus didn't die for groups; He died for individuals. There is an emphasis throughout the Scripture on the individual, and this Biblical emphasis on the individual was a core feature of our political philosophy. There have always been those who preferred to and who attempted to elevate the group above the individual, but the Bible always turns the focus to the individual.

Consider how this is illustrated by the Bible-minded Pilgrims — one of the earliest advocates for equal civil rights. When a boat load of slaves arrived at their colony, they freed the slaves and imprisoned the slave-owners — and there never was a time in Massachusetts when blacks could not vote. The Pilgrims embraced the simple Bible-based philosophy that there were really only two people groups, and those groups were not identified by race, ethnicity, geography, or any other superficial distinction. The two groups recognized by the Pilgrims were those who knew God and those who didn't. It was the individual and his relationship with God that mattered most. This view also affected their relationships with the neighboring Indians, resulting in the longest-lasting treaty with Native Americans in American history.

Similarly, when the Founding Fathers drafted the Bill of Rights, they provided protection for the inalienable rights of every individual, regardless of the group to which they belonged. But today, as groups have become more important than individuals, the Constitution and Bill of Rights have been reinterpreted, causing many courts to now claim that the Bill of Rights is designed to protect the minority from the majority — that is, to protect one group from another group. But consider the absurdity of this view. Does this therefore mean that an individual loses his right of free speech, self-defense, freedom of religion, and trial by jury if he happens to be an Anglo, a male, a Christian, or a Democrat — all of whom are considered, statistically speaking, to be in the majority? Of course not. The Bill of Rights was designed to protect the inalienable rights of every individual, regardless of the group of which he or she may be a part.

Question #2: How can I get a reliable view of history?

In our nation's first three centuries, truth was the highest objective — seek the truth and tell the truth. Truth was not to be sacrificed to any agenda; the end did not justify the means. Those who believed otherwise were considered scoundrels. But today, as America has become more and more secular, achieving particular outcomes matters more than pursuing truth, so certain aspects of truth are withheld if they impede a desired result. Thus, for secularists who seek a secular society, it is acceptable to withhold from students a knowledge of the positive influence of the Bible and Christianity upon America and even to deny that those influences ever existed.

One technique that counters this, and that helps produce a sound and factually-balanced presentation of history, is presented in the Bible: it is the use of biographical history. So, if you want you learn about the Philistines, you read the stories of Samuel, Saul, and David — you study the biographies of these individuals. Biographical history also helps us use our imagination: we place ourselves in their shoes, and we see what they did and why — we learn about their character, and their strengths and weaknesses. In short, we learn lessons from centuries and even millennia ago that still apply today.

SESSION 8

STUDY GUIDE

For generations in America, we learned American history the same way. We thus studied the biographies of George Washington, Abigail Adams, James Otis, and James Armistead to learn about the principles of liberty and the American Revolution; we learned about the progress of science by studying Benjamin Franklin, David Rittenhouse, George Washington Carver, and Thomas Edison; we studied the Civil War and the fight for civil rights by learning about the life and struggles of Abraham Lincoln, Robert E. Lee, Robert Small, and Harriet Tubman; and so forth. This long-established custom of learning history by studying the lives of its heroes has fallen into disfavor over the past half-century, but the use of biographical history helps overcome Poststructuralism, Anti-nationalism, Deconstructionism, and Negativism.

So, if you want to get a good view and understanding of early American history, you can read the 1818 book *Sketches of the Life of Patrick Henry* by William Wirt, the Attorney General of the United States and a strong Christian; and the 1839 *Life of George Washington* by Jared Sparks, an early chaplain of Congress and president of Harvard; and the 1849 *Life and Public Services of John Quincy Adams* by Christian statesman William Seward; and so forth. You can also ready Founding Father Noah Webster's 1832 *History of the United States* and Founding Father David Ramsay's 1789 *History of the American Revolution*, and other similar works. The more you use original sources, the more accurate will be the history that you read. Today, it is a sad reality that many biographers deliberately omit the religious beliefs and motivations of the historic individuals about whom they write, but this was not the case with older works.

(Hundreds of thousands of these old books and biographies are now available online, without cost, and can often be downloaded as pdfs — such as at Books.Google.com. Historical links on Wallbuilders.com (WallBuilders.com/links.asp) also provide links to several other sites filled with original historical documents and writings; and WallBuilders.com also has an extensive collection of such documents and writings.)

SESSION

STUDY GUIDE

Question #3: Isn't it arrogant for Americans to say we're exceptional? Aren't all men created equal?

To look at a team in any particular sport and declare that one team in that sport is better than the others isn't arrogance so long as it's based on a factual, statistical record. It is not arrogant to report the truth, but it is arrogant to conceitedly declare "I'm better and worth more than you are." But we're not exceptional simply because we're Americans; rather, it's that the timeless principles we adopted are exceptional, and it is these principles that made America (and can make any other nation) exceptional when embraced and applied.

> *"Therefore the Lord God of Israel says: 'I said indeed that your house and the house of your father would walk before Me forever.' But now the Lord says: 'Far be it from Me; for those who honor Me I will honor, and those who despise Me shall be lightly esteemed."*
>
> — 1 Samuel 2:30

> *"It must be felt that there is no national security but in the nation's humble, acknowledged dependence upon God and His overruling Providence."*
> — President Franklin Pierce

Question #4: America's greatness seems to be slipping. How do we save our exceptionalism?

The five principles set forth in the Declaration that produced our exceptionalism must become fundamental to the way we think and approach our government. We can no longer measure the effectiveness of government and select our leaders based solely on our pocketbooks or other economic considerations. Instead, we must choose our leaders on the basis of whether they will preserve and perpetuate, or attack or weaken the foundations that have caused America to become unique among the nations of the world.

> *"If the foundations be destroyed, what shall the righteous do?"*
>
> — Psalms 11:3

The key to restoring our exceptionalism is:

- Know what caused our exceptionalism
- Go back and rediscover an unbiased American history — learn what made us a great nation

- Get rid of the Deconstructionism and Poststructuralism that separates, criticizes, and promotes negativity. We are to tell the good, the bad, and the ugly, and we therefore mustn't omit the good about America, as has become common practice today. Romans 12:21 says to overcome the evil with the good, so take time to learn the good things about America; you probably have already been told the bad things!
- Teach the five principles of American Exceptionalism to others, and elect to office those who embrace and will implement those principles.

 ADDITIONAL READING/VIEWING/LISTENING

- *Keeping Truth in History* by David Barton
- *Principles of National Reformation* by David Barton
- *Exceptional!* by David Barton
- *The Founders' Bible* by David Barton

 DISCUSSION QUESTIONS AFTER WATCHING THE VIDEO

1. How would you define American Exceptionalism?

American Exceptionalism describes the unprecedented freedom, stability, and prosperity that are the result of institutions and policies produced by a unique governing philosophy.

2. Why is Poststructuralism/Anti-nationalism so dangerous to our existence as a nation?

Focusing on groups rather than individuals causes us to sacrifice the individual to the group, thus negating recognition of and protection for our God-given inalienable rights. The principles of freedom and prosperity are applicable to every person, regardless of any demographic distinctions. Groups cultivate an "us vs. them" mentality and disrupt national unity, and as Jesus affirmed, "A house divided against itself cannot stand" (Mark 3:25).

8 SESSION

STUDY GUIDE

3. What are some ways you can personally counter the attacks on American Exceptionalism?

- Memorize the five principles that produce American Exceptionalism
- Educate yourself about America's true history
- Educate others about the five principles of American Exceptionalism and about sound American history; explain to them why individuals are more important than groups
- Make a conscious effort to focus on and promote individuals rather than groups
- Work with your school board, and elect good officials who will ensure that original historical sources and documents are being used in the classroom

Session 9

CHANGING A STATE — AND A GENERATION

"The preservation of the means of knowledge among the lowest ranks is of more importance to the public than all the property of all the rich men in the country."

— John Adams

CHANGING A STATE — AND A GENERATION

INTRODUCTION

Why does it seem like the majority of people in government today are pushing for the wrong policies? It is because of what they were taught in school. As Abraham Lincoln wisely acknowledged, "The philosophy of the schoolroom in one generation will be the philosophy of government in the next." So what can be done to reverse what is now being taught in the classroom and subsequently implemented into public policy?

There is definitely a solution available, but it is not a quick fix. Too often, Christian activists want to see all problems corrected immediately (if not sooner), and they thus have very little patience with what often seems to them only to be meager gains or victories. However, to be truly effective, we must adopt a long-term vision and strategy and embrace all progress, no matter how great or how small it may seem.

Today's lesson will explore the forgotten battlefield of tomorrow's government policy: the public school classroom, which is one of the most important arenas for long-term activism and involvement. This is true for all citizens, regardless of whether or not they have children in those schools. Some 88% of America's students attend government schools, and many of those students will become our leaders. So because what those students are being taught today will determine how they approach public policy tomorrow, citizens must engage in that battlefield of ideas.

In today's session, you'll learn:

- The impact of education on government
- How one state turned their history curriculum around — and the impact it can have on the rest of the country
- What you can do to impact your state's education system
- Why a long-term view of involvement is the Biblical approach to change
- Who should be active in reforming public education

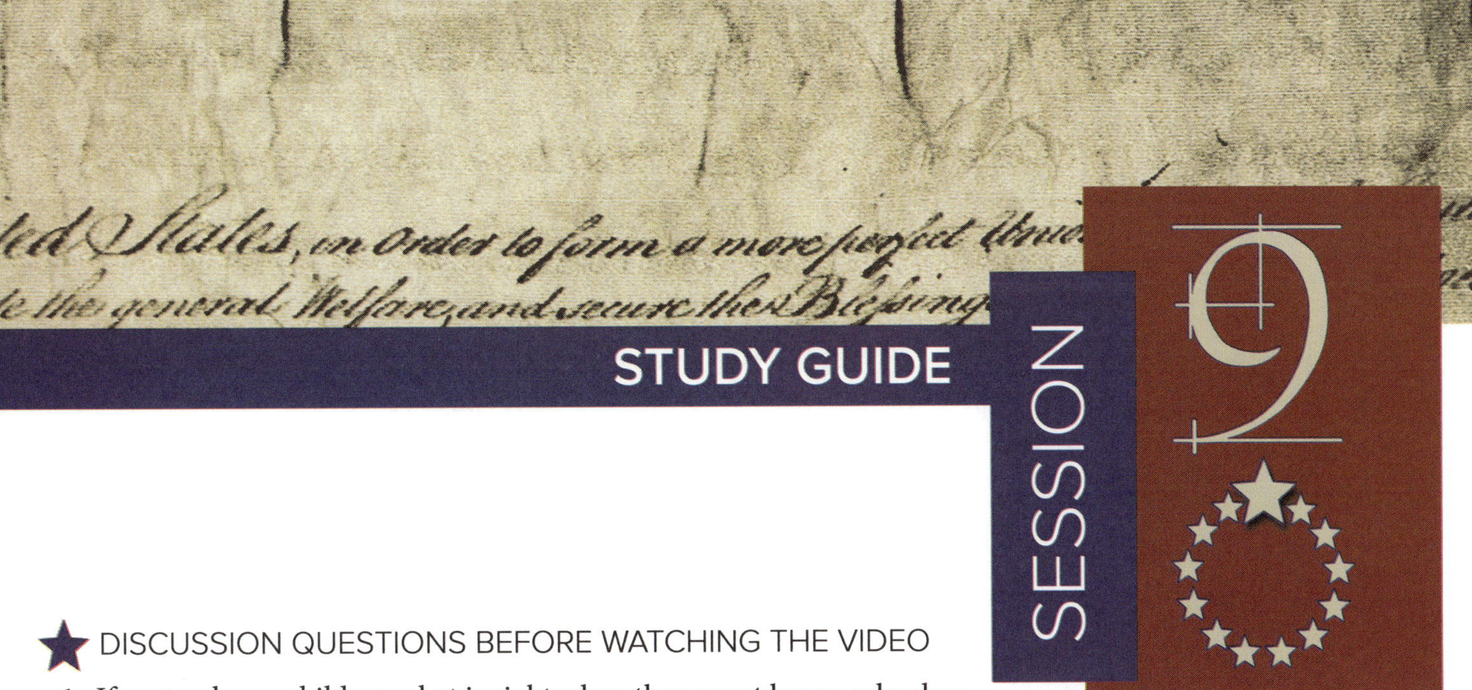

★ DISCUSSION QUESTIONS BEFORE WATCHING THE VIDEO

1. If we teach our children what is right when they are at home, why does it matter what they are taught at school?
2. Should we be involved with government schools if our own children don't attend there?
3. Why have our schools become such concentrated centers of intense anti-Biblical values?

Who determines the philosophy that will be taught in the classroom? There are many who have influence on that decision, and from bottom to top some of the key ones are:

- active citizens
- classroom teachers and superintendents
- local school boards
- textbooks and curriculum
- state laws and state education agency mandates
- federal laws and federal Department of Education mandates

> *"'Tis education forms*
> *The common mind,*
> *Just as the twig is bent,*
> *The tree's inclined."*
> — Alexander Pope, 1734,
> Epistle to Cobham

We should always be very concerned about both the content and the philosophy of local education, which are largely inculcated through curricular content. Every state creates curriculum standards setting forth the minimum content of what children in their state must learn, and these standards determine what is then placed into student textbooks.

Significantly, for decades, the textbook standards from Texas and California have driven the textbook content for all states. This is because national publishers invest millions to produce a textbook, and to recoup that high cost there must be enough students in a state to whom that textbook can be sold. Texas and California have about one-fourth of the nation's students, so if publishers conform to the standards in those two states, and can sell their textbooks there, they can recover their costs. So even though states such as North Dakota, Oklahoma, South Carolina, and others create their own standards for their students, few publishers will produce a textbook exclusively for these less populous states. (Of course, this changes with online curriculums, which can be produced and modified at a much lower expense.)

Interestingly, the recent American History standards proposed by classroom educators in Texas were filled with content reflecting intense Revisionism and extreme Poststructuralism (i.e., identifying people by their groups rather than as individuals), and many of the positive things about America were also missing. But when the State Board of Education reviewed those proposed standards, they overrode the teachers and rejected both the negative tone and the Revisionism, insisting instead on teaching American Exceptionalism. The State Board made over 200 positive changes in the standards.

Significantly, these wholesome changes passed the State Board by a wide margin of 11-4, but just a few years earlier, the Board rejected similar changes by a margin of 14 to 1. That is an overall shift of ten votes. How did such a change occur? It required a decade of hard work by citizens behind the scenes.

It began with actively recruiting good individuals who had the right values and philosophy and then working to get them elected. So in one election cycle, there might be an increase of perhaps only 3 good votes; but in the next election, maybe 2 more were added; and then in the following election maybe another 2; but along the way, some of the good ones retired, so the next election added perhaps 3 more good votes, but some were only replacements for the retiring good votes. It was a slow and arduous task.

Nonetheless, by making and keeping these educational positions an emphasis, over the course of a decade the Texas State Board of Education gained enough solid votes to ensure that sound American History would be taught — and also that the evolution-only secularist science philosophy would not be coerced onto students; that sex education would promote sexual abstinence rather than promiscuity; and so forth with other subjects.

SESSION 

STUDY GUIDE

As a result of what occurred in Texas, and because of the great influence of Texas on national textbook content, the entire nation has benefitted from those unheralded folks in Texas — from the citizen leaders who recruited the candidates, ran the campaigns, cast the votes, and served in office.

To arrive at this point and achieve this victory took years of dedicated, unrelenting, focused work, but this incremental approach of gaining a little at a time is actually the Biblical means for victory and lasting change. What happened to the Texas State Board is a model that can be replicated anywhere, at either a state or a local level.

> ***"I will not drive them out in a single year. Little by little I will drive them out before you."***
>
> – Exodus 23:29-30

> ***"The Lord your God will drive them out from before you little by little. You will not be allowed to eliminate them all at once."***
>
> – Deuteronomy 7:22

There are numerous other things that states and communities can do to help improve both the philosophy and content of education, particularly in the area of American History:

- Create American History standards with sound content that teaches the good as well as the bad and the ugly, that also present wholesome heroes, that include the important role of faith and the Bible, and that rely heavily upon original documents.
- Adopt textbooks whose content reflects these standards
- Enact "Celebrate Freedom Week" policies, requiring students from Grades 3-12 to spend one week each year reading and studying the Declaration of Independence, the Constitution, and the Bill of Rights.
- Observe Constitution Day. Federal law requires that each September 17, schools must honor this day by dedicating time to reading and studying the Constitution. Currently, only 10% of schools comply with this law. Make sure your school does — and find and recommend a good curriculum for them to use on Constitution Day (there are many available).

- Stay connected with your local school board — visit with and get to know its members — and ensure that they adopt good content and follow these laws. If they do not, copy the Texas model and begin to steadily recruit and gradually elect to the school board those who will implement wholesome practices. If necessary, run for office yourself.
- In addition to securing good content and textbooks for American History, also monitor and stay involved with the other textbook content standards for other subjects. Such standards are usually adopted at the state level, but also at the school district level, especially in larger districts.

Question #1: Shouldn't we leave education to the experts?

What is an expert, and how do you identify one? An "expert" should be determined not by the degree or title they hold but rather by their performance. For example, more than a dozen U. S. Presidents did not hold a college degree; so were they unqualified for that important position? In fact, 2 of the 4 presidents whose faces appear on Mount Rushmore (George Washington and Abraham Lincoln) did not have a college degree, and they are widely regarded as two of America's best presidents, but neither would have been considered a political or governmental expert.

Similarly, only around 10% percent of homeschool parents have a degree in education, which thus makes them an "expert" in teaching children. Yet homeschool children average 2-4 grade levels higher on academic tests than do their public school counterparts. So nearly 90% of homeschool parents are not "experts," yet the children they teach academically learn much more than those children taught only by the so-called "experts." This is not to disparage credentialed teachers but rather to say that it is not credentials alone that create an "expert."

In fact, American education has been in the hands of experts for the past several decades, and our educational measurements have plummeted. In international testing in math and science, we regularly are at the bottom; and 19% of each year's graduates are completely illiterate. The "experts" and their current philosophy are definitely not producing the results widely experienced in previous years. We need to get away from placing an emphasis on titles and return to what works.

Question #2: I've tried voting, and even volunteering, but it didn't make a difference. Why should I put forth the effort if I don't see results?

Citizens must put forth the effort and stay involved, not because they see a certain set of results but simply because it's the right thing to do. A lesson from signer of the Declaration Benjamin Rush is appropriate here. Considered the greatest physician in American history, Rush was also a strong Christian leader, having started the Sunday School movement in America as well as the first Bible Society. And he was a leader in numerous humanitarian efforts — faith-based reforms in prisons; medical reforms for the mentally ill; the abolition of slavery and civil rights for all Americans, regardless of race; academic education for women, and many others worthy endeavors. But despite his dedicated efforts, slavery remained; prisoners often went unreformed; and medical practices frequently did not produce the desired results. Understandably, he was frustrated. Contemplating his many apparent failures and unachieved goals, in his memoirs he reported:

> "Upon my complaining at another time of the abortive issue of many of my plans for promoting the happiness of my fellow citizens, he [a minister friend] said, 'Don't be uneasy upon that account. Our Savior will say at the Day of Judgment, "Well done thou faithful, not thou successful, servant" [Matthew 25:21]. Let this comfort you under all your disappointments. If you have been faithful, it will be enough.'"

Many of the objectives Rush sought were not immediately realized, but his unrelenting efforts paved the way for many others to pick up the torches he had carried by himself for so long. Ultimately, many of his reforms were finally implemented by those who later caught his vision and followed his example.

> ***"His lord said to him, 'Well done, good and faithful servant; you were faithful over a few things, I will make you ruler over many things. Enter into the joy of your lord.'"***
>
> — Matthew 25:21

STUDY GUIDE

"And let us not grow weary while doing good, for in due season we shall reap if we do not lose heart."

— Galatians 6:9

Always remember that elections are not absolute events but rather are part of a lifelong process. Don't give up in your efforts, even if you are the only one engaged. If you have no good candidates to vote for, then go upstream and start recruiting some good ones. By the way, if you simply wait for someone good to step forward, usually very few ever will. (For a Biblical explanation of this phenomenon, see Judges 9.) So work hard to recruit better candidates for the future while doing all that you can in elections right now.

Question #3: So many of my friends, and the families in my church, either homeschool or go to private school. Why should we bother with the public schools or their textbook process?

The reason that those with children in private or homeschool should be concerned about those who aren't is that most of the people who rule over us do not come from private or homeschool. Maybe someday they will (after all, George Washington, Benjamin Franklin, John Jay, Patrick Henry, and other significant leaders in the Founding Era were homeschooled), but right now, that's not the realm from which most future leaders come.

"Always drink on the upstream side of the horses."
— Old Cowboy Axiom

Furthermore, we all pay hard-earned taxes to finance the public education system. So regardless of where we send our own children — and even if we don't have children — we should always seek to get the best return on our investment. As a taxpayer, you always have what is called "taxpayer standing," which means that as long as you are paying taxes, you have the legal right to participate in the decisions made in the public school system, whether you personally use the system or not.

In addition to securing good content and electing sound leaders, there are many other things that can be done to help change school policy and philosophy. For example, unanimous decisions from the Supreme Court authorize Bible clubs, evangelism clubs, prayer clubs, and the like in public schools. So start a Bible or evangelism club, or a prayer club for students.

And students in public schools can also have a for-credit course with the Bible as the course textbook. The National Council on Bible Curriculum in Public Schools provides curriculum for this course. The courts have upheld it, and it is currently being taught in more than a thousand school districts to tens of thousands of students.

National Council on Bible Curriculum in Public Schools
BibleInSchools.net

You can also start Christian Good New Clubs at schools around you. These are Christian clubs for elementary students. The courts routinely uphold these clubs, and even school teachers can lead them. (Good News Clubs: cfonline.com) Courts also uphold Released Time, where students can be released from school for an hour a week to attend religious classes. Many churches obtain a room near the school, using that hour to teach students the Bible, doctrine, apologetics, worldview, or whatever. (Released Time Education: rtce.org)

So, there are many things you can do to improve both the philosophy and content of education in public schools.

 ADDITIONAL READING/VIEWING/LISTENING

- *Keeping Truth in History* by David Barton
- *Four Centuries of American Education* by David Barton
- *Common Core* by David Barton
- *A Nation Adrift* by Timothy Barton
- *Drive thru History America* curriculum (available from WallBuilders.com)

9 SESSION STUDY GUIDE

★ DISCUSSION QUESTIONS AFTER WATCHING THE VIDEO

1. Can I influence the public school system by leaving my children in it to be missionaries?

Children are only students in the public school system, they are not the teachers. They therefore receive, they don't give — they follow policy, they don't make it. It is possible they might have some influence on their peers, but the system, the curriculum, and the philosophy — which are the most important elements in any school — are determined by adults. This is why adults have to be involved with public schools, regardless of where their own children go. Don't endanger or sacrifice your children by exposing them to worldview and morals and philosophies that may destroy their spirit or a proper view of America. We need to get involved ourselves rather than send our children unprotected and vulnerable into the lion's den — it is voters, school board members, and those within the inner workings of the education system who can best influence the system.

2. Why is history so important?

The Bible teaches us that the way that a people views it history will affect the way that people behaves. For this reason, the Bible admonishes us in numerous passages to know history. For example:

- Remember the days of old, consider the years of many generations; ask thy father, and he will show thee; thy elders, and they will tell thee. (Deuteronomy 32:7)
- I have considered the days of old, the years of ancient times. (Psalm 77:5)
- Remember the former things of old. (Isaiah 46:9)
- For whatsoever things were written aforetime were written for our learning. (Romans 15:4)
- Call to remembrance the former days. (Hebrews 10:32)

(For verses with a similar emphasis, see Psalm 78:1-7; Psalm 105 & Psalm 106; Deuteronomy 4:32; Job 8:7-8; Ecclesiastes 1:9-11; 1 Corinthians 10:1, 11; and others.)

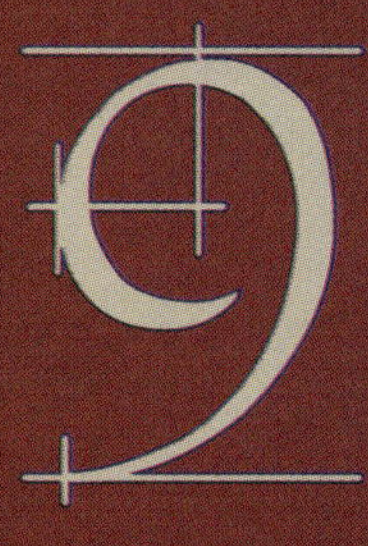

Our leaders' governmental philosophy is most influenced by their understanding of American history. If they have a favorable and accurate view of America and what made it exceptional, then they are more likely to work to preserve those principles in the public policy decisions they make.

3. What are some ways you can impact the education system?

- Become active in local school affairs, monitoring content, curriculum, and policy
- Work to ensure that your local school has the best leadership possible. If it doesn't, then recruit and run good leadership for office — or if need be, run for office yourself
- Attend school board meetings and blog for others about what was covered in the meetings, keeping them informed of what is occurring, whether good or bad
- Lobby local schools to teach the Constitution on Constitution Day and to adopt Celebrate Freedom Week
- Help begin good elective classes, such as those on the Bible, or start clubs that provide students a way to express and strengthen their faith while in the midst of an the overtly secularist system of government schools

SESSION 10

REVIVAL AND REFORMATION

"And have we now forgotten that powerful Friend? Or do we imagine we no longer need His assistance? I have lived, sir, a long time; and the longer I live, the more convincing proofs I see of this truth: that God governs in the affairs of men. And if a sparrow cannot fall to the ground without His notice, is it probable that an empire can rise without His aid?"

— Benjamin Franklin

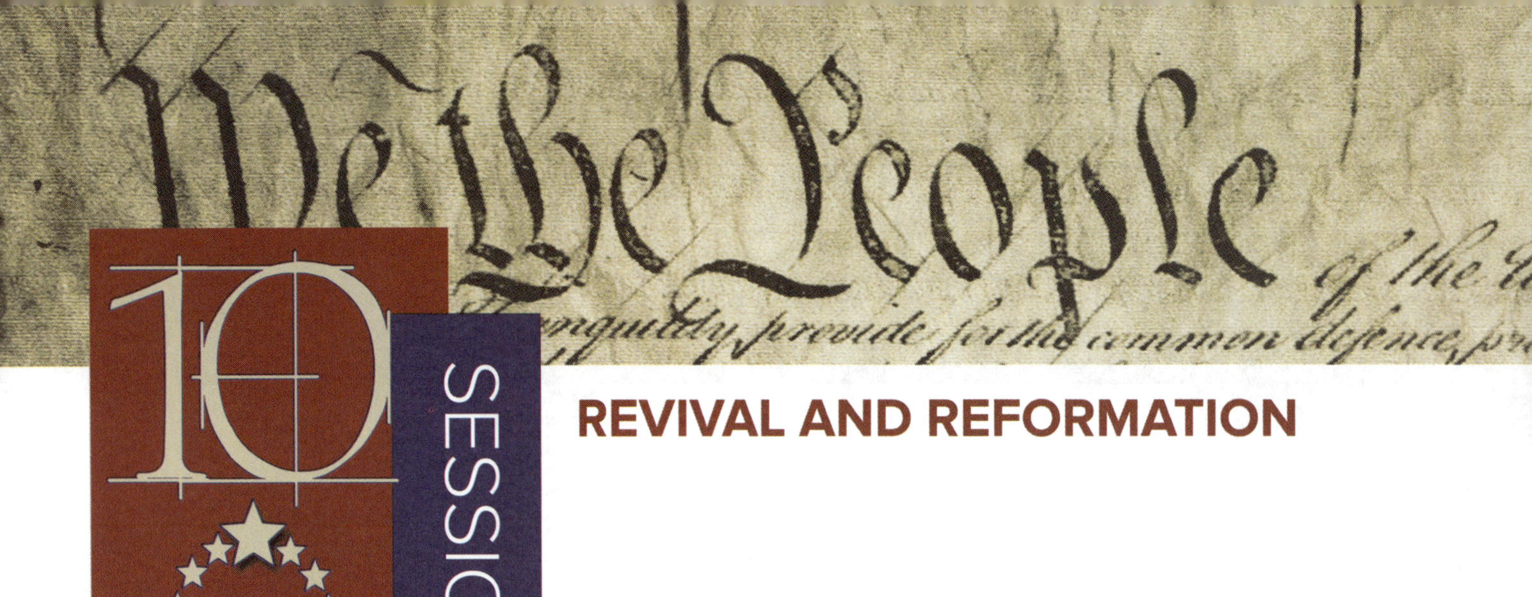

REVIVAL AND REFORMATION

INTRODUCTION

We often hear today that what our country really needs is revival. But what is a revival — and what does it mean to have a revival? And is a revival (as most think of it today) really the key to turning our country around?

Throughout history, revivals have impacted, altered, and transformed the course of nations. This has certainly been true in America. For example, the seeds planted in the First Great Awakening ripened into the harvest of the American Revolution, providing freedom, a new form of government, and a distinctly different culture for the entire nation. And the Second Great Awakening led to the end of slavery and produced other positive lasting changes.

History shows that over and over, nations suffering from moral decay and corruption have been turned around by revival. But true revival requires much hard work, involves unexpectedly intense opposition from religious leaders, and can take years to come to completion; but the fruit it produces in the lives of individuals can restore a nation to being a God-honoring society.

In today's lesson, you'll learn:

- How to recognize a real revival
- How revivals have impacted American history
- How to initiate revival

DISCUSSION QUESTIONS BEFORE WATCHING THE VIDEO

1. What is revival?
2. Why hasn't God sent revival to America in over a century?
3. Has America gone too far down the road of no return for a revival to save the country?

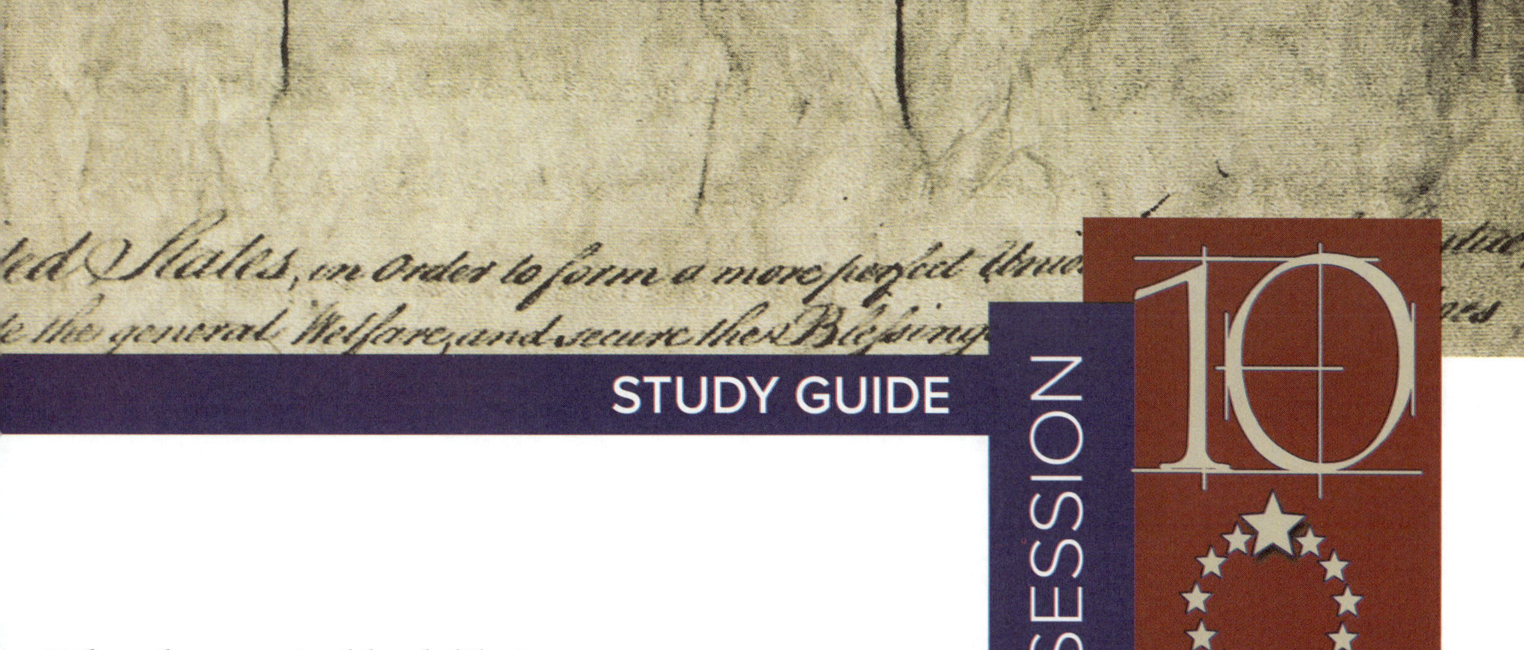

What does revival look like?

1. Significantly, revivals are not fast-moving events that immediately transform a nation; rather, they are slow and steady movements of God that cover decades.

The First Great Awakening lasted 40 years, generally spanning the period from 1730 to 1770. The Second Great Awakening is considered to have run from as early as 1801 to as late as 1878 — 77 years. Because of the long duration of true revivals, usually those who are in a revival don't realize they are; it is generally historians who, years later, recognize what happened as a move of God and then long after the fact label it as a revival.

From the historical standpoint, a revival is not something that suddenly moves in and sweeps through a country over a weekend, with Americans waking up on Monday morning, having dedicated themselves and the nation to going in a new, Godly direction. Instead, a revival always requires much hard and prolonged work.

The Rev. George Whitefield is perhaps the most recognizable name from the First Great Awakening and the man most closely associated with that national revival. Arriving from England, he made more than half-a-dozen missionary journeys across America (on horseback) preaching everywhere he went. In fact, during his more than three decades of ministry in America, he preached over 18,000 sermons — an average of more than two every day. And between sermons, he rode his horse from town to town, attempting to reach every corner of America — which he almost did. It is estimated that 80% of Americans actually heard him preach a sermon. That revival required rigorously hard work, and the demands literally killed him — the rough life and tough schedule took its toll on him bodily and eventually resulted in his death. Great personal sacrifice is what was required to produce the revival that in turn produced the lasting cultural changes that blessed so many millions.

And while Whitefield was a famous national face of revival, the revival was in reality largely conducted region by region, and city by city across America. Thus, there was the Rev. Samuel Davies working in Virginia; the Rev. Gilbert Tennant in Pennsylvania; the Rev. Harry Hoosier in Indiana; the Rev. Jonathan Mayhew in Boston; the Rev. Jonathan Edwards in Massachusetts; and so forth. Each of them embraced and engaged in the hard and tedious work required for a revival.

"In 1739 arrived among us from Ireland the Reverend Mr. Whitefield, who had made himself remarkable there as an itinerant preacher. He was at first permitted to preach in some of our churches; but the clergy, taking a dislike to him, soon refus'd him their pulpits, and he was oblig'd to preach in the fields....It was wonderful to see the change soon made in the manners of our inhabitants. From being thoughtless or indifferent about religion, it seem'd as if all the world were growing religious, so that one could not walk thro' the town in an evening without hearing psalms sung in different families of every street."
— Benjamin Franklin, *The Autobiography of Benjamin Franklin*

2. Revivals are always characterized by opposition from the spiritual people, not just the secular folks.

During the Great Awakening, religious leaders heavily criticized Whitefield because what he did differed dramatically from their comfortable traditions. After all, he held meetings in open fields and invited hearers from all denominations and races, and most of what he did occurred outside the organized structure of the traditional church. Several prominent ministers therefore published vicious writings against him, condemning and openly attacking him, disparaging his doctrines and meetings and the manner in which his services were conducted. The published criticisms often followed the tone of, "This is not the way we do things." "We've never done it this way before." "He's introduced new and different things that we're not accustomed to." Many of the pious Christian laity also joined the opposition to Whitefield, with some standing in trees and urinating on him while he spoke, and others pelting him with rotted fruit.

Significantly, when God decides to sovereignly move, it is often in ways that offend and distress His people. In the New Testament, when God chose to include the Gentiles, the Apostles were highly offended. When Jesus sat down at the well with a Samaritan woman, His disciples criticized Him, because Jews had an intense loathing for Samaritans — they were the scum of the earth. But Jesus even went so far as to make the Good Samaritan the hero of the story rather than Jewish priests or Levite leaders. So, when a true spiritual movement begins, it often offends religious folk.

It was also this way with the Second Great Awakening, which treated men and women, blacks and whites as equals. Revival leaders such as Charles Finney, Lorenzo Dow, and others were attacked by pastors and church-goers alike for daring to act on verses such as Galatians 3:28 ("There is neither Jew nor Gentile, neither slave nor free, nor is there male and female, for you are all one in Christ Jesus") and for extending equality to all, without regard to physical or other superficial distinctions.

Jesus summarized the primary problem that arises during a revival when he talked about the old and new wineskins — He wants to do new and different things, but the old wineskins usually can't handle it (Luke 5:36-38). So strive to be a new wineskin — be open to new and unexpected methods of how God might choose to work. If it is a revival, it will probably occur outside the scope of what you expect; it might well make you very uncomfortable.

In short, if you are praying for a revival and want to be part of it, then expect intense and active opposition from both religious leaders and laymen who will firmly oppose what God is doing, and especially the way in which (and through whom) He chooses to manifest Himself.

3. Revival is not just a spiritual movement.

Another characteristic of a revival is that it involves a practical application of Biblical faith to day to day life, and in realms far outside of what is typically considered to be spiritual. The early American church believed that God's word provided guidance for every issue of life — that there was no topic of life to which Biblical principles could not be successfully applied. Sermons from America's previous revivals clearly illustrate this, for when something big was in the news, it was often covered in the pulpit as well, being presented from a Biblical perspective. The Church thus taught the nation a practical Christianity.

"In Suits at common law, where the value in controversy shall exceed twenty dollars, the right of trial by jury shall be preserved, and no fact tried by a jury, shall be otherwise re-examined in any Court of the United States, than according to the rules of the common law."
— Amendment VII of the Constitution

For example, when New England suffered an earthquake in 1755, sermons followed that event addressing earthquakes. In 1760, sermons addressed the Great Fire in Boston. And "Execution Sermons" were also preached whenever a prisoner was executed by government. Other sermons from those revivals addressed:

- Technology, including railroads, shipping, and the transatlantic cable
- Architecture and the completion of a bridge

- Science and astronomy, including sermons on solar eclipses, comets, the discovery of a new planet, snow, and vapor
- Laws addressing marriage, economics, taxes, or crime
- National defense issues and foreign affairs
- Christian citizenship and ways to preserve the Constitution
- Social benevolence and helping the poor and needy
- Issues touching health and aging
- Education and learning
- Civil government and elections
- Alcohol abuse, dueling, slavery, gambling, profanity, and whatever else was a controversial social or moral issue of the day

John Adams specifically praised these types of sermons:

> It is the duty of the clergy to accommodate their discourses to the times — to preach against such sins as are most prevalent and recommend such virtues as are most wanted [lacking]. For example, if exorbitant ambition and venality [public corruption and bribery] are predominant, ought they not to warn their hearers against these vices? If public spirit [service and patriotism] is much wanted [lacking], should they not inculcate this great virtue? If the rights and duties of Christian magistrates [public officials] and subjects are disputed, should they not explain them, show their nature, ends, limitations, and restrictions, how much soever it may move the gall [irritate the critics]?

Why are such sermons not delivered today? It certainly is not because the Bible is silent about these issues or that it does not have principles that apply. It is just that today we have become so compartmentalized that we limit Christianity just to so-called pre-conceived "spiritual" things rather than real life. But a revival makes Biblical faith practical to every area of life.

4. Revivals are usually transgenerational.

God often answers prayers for revival by sending a new generation that does things differently, restoring the nation and culture back to God.

SESSION 10

STUDY GUIDE

Significantly, many of the noted political and military leaders of the American Revolution had been greatly influenced in their youth by famous preachers from the Great Awakening. For example:

- Rev. Samuel Davies, the greatest pulpit orator in American history, directly influenced a young Patrick Henry, who subsequently became a great political orator.
- Rev. Samuel Cooper similarly influenced a young John Quincy Adams.
- Rev. Gilbert Tennent likewise shaped a young Benjamin Rush, a signer of the Declaration whom John Adams labeled as being one of America's three most notable Founding Fathers.

And there are many other examples.

Question #1: What will it take to get revival in America?

You have to start by asking God for revival, and that means you have to start with prayer. But prayer will not be enough. The more you pray for something, the more your heart will be turned toward that particular thing, and the more likely you are to take action accordingly. For example, God tells us to pray "first of all" for our civil leaders and those in authority. But if you obey the Scripture and pray diligently for your leaders, you will find that prayer won't be enough. Your prayer will cause you to become motivated to take action and become involved with your leaders in some way. So, too, with praying for revival.

> ***"Therefore I exhort first of all that supplications, prayers, intercessions, and giving of thanks be made for all men, for kings and all who are in authority, that we may lead a quiet and peaceable life in all godliness and reverence."***
>
> – I Timothy 2:1-2

You should pray fervently for revival, but if you're not willing to do something along with your prayers, then revival is not going to happen. You must engage the culture and take stands in line with what you are praying for. And when you do so in a culture that needs revival, you can expect to be disliked and attacked. You may become unpopular, but you must have backbone and not back down, regardless of the pressure. And you must also become comfortable with working long and hard. All of this

> *"Again the children of Israel did evil in the sight of the Lord, and the Lord delivered them into the hand of the Philistines for forty years. Now there was a certain man...whose name was Manoah; and his wife was barren and had no children. And the Angel of the Lord appeared to the woman and said to her, '...behold, you shall conceive and bear a son....and he shall begin to deliver Israel out of the hand of the Philistines.'"*
>
> — Judges 13: 1-5

> *"I was first taught what an orator should be by listening to Davies preach."*
>
> — Patrick Henry

> *"I urge you, by the all that is dear, by all that is honorable, by all that is sacred, not only that ye pray, but that ye act."*
>
> — John Hancock

is associated with revival, and if we are not willing to do this, it is unlikely that revival will come.

> ***"If the world hates you, keep in mind that it hated Me first. If you belonged to the world, it would love you as its own. As it is, you do not belong to the world, but I have chosen you out of the world. That is why the world hates you. Remember what I told you: 'A servant is not greater than his master.' If they persecuted Me, they will persecute you also. If they obeyed My teaching, they will obey yours also."***
>
> — John 15:18-20

Question #2: How do we measure revival?

Revival is measured by changes in individuals, which eventually produces change in the culture. But unless individuals get a strong enough dose of Christianity to cause them to embrace and live by Biblical attitudes and values in every aspect of their lives, the culture will not change.

Interestingly, the Bible records national revivals under Josiah, Asa, and Jeshophat. A factor common to each was that when a spiritual awakening occurred, there was a change in attitude toward sexual licentiousness and homosexuality — the toleration for and acceptance of that behavior went down.

> ***"And he [Asa] took away the sodomites out of the land..."***
>
> — 1 Kings 15:12

> ***"And the remnant of the sodomites, which remained in the days of his father Asa, he [Jehoshaphat] took out of the land."***
>
> — 1 Kings 22:46

> ***"And he [Josiah] brake down the houses of the sodomites that were by the house of the Lord."***
>
> — 2 Kings 23:7

A spiritual movement is not a true revival unless it gets outside the church and affects the culture and its policies, impacting national institutions such as education, media, business, law, and government.

Question #3: America is so far down the wrong road and is moving so rapidly in the wrong direction that it seems we have only a few years left. How can we get revival in such a short time?

Every generation since Christ was on earth thought that He would return in their generation and thus felt the pressure of shortness of time. Of course, so far all previous generations have been wrong. This generation, like every one before it, also believes in a shortness of time, but if we in this generation think that now is the time to get out of here because the going has gotten rough, then not only have we not yet developed strong and mature Christian character but we are still unaware of several major Bible teachings, including Jesus' direct command to "Occupy 'till I come" (Luke 19:13).

Furthermore, across the pages of the Bible, Israel repeatedly turned against God, openly rejecting Him, even persecuting and killing those who followed His teachings and values. In many areas they were much further over the cliff than America is now. But whenever the nation decided to turn back to Him, He brought them back from the brink and restored them to greatness. In fact, several times throughout the Bible, even though God had decreed a certain outcome for a person or a nation, as a result of prayer God changed what He intended to do. So America definitely is not too far gone — if we are willing to pray and do our part. But we must stand and face the opposition, not turn and run and ask for God to take us out of here.

> ***"Surely the arm of the Lord is not too short to save, nor His ear too dull to hear."***
>
> — Isaiah 59:1

10 SESSION

STUDY GUIDE

 ADDITIONAL READING/VIEWING/LISTENING

- *Principles of National Reformation* by David Barton
- *The Role of Pastors and Christians in Civil Government/Foundations of American Government* by David Barton
- *The Founders' Bible* by David Barton

 DISCUSSION QUESTIONS AFTER WATCHING THE VIDEO

1. How is revival different from what we typically think it is?

We tend to think that revival is when the Holy Spirit suddenly swoops in, takes over, and supernaturally fixes the problems. We often consider it as an almost-magical phenomenon that suspends time and space — an event with no rhyme or reason — something mysterious. But to the contrary, revival is governed by spiritual laws and principles just as real as physical laws and principles. Revival always takes much longer than we think it will, and the work is much harder, and goes much deeper — it is not something superficial and quick but rather it goes to the roots. It transforms not only lives and communities but also the society and government. And not all professing Christians will welcome revival (although they probably will not recognize it for what it is when it arrives), and folks usually don't know they are in a revival until historians later tell them. Many times Christians will actively oppose a revival because of how different it is from what they have grown accustomed to.

2. What is something important we can do to bring about revival?

First, get spiritually hungry. Pray. Read and apply God's Word. Don't make the Bible just an add-on to your life, but rather make it the core of your life — something from which all else flows. God is the only One Who can send revival, and He wants to do it more than we could ever want it. But it involves action — we have to act out our faith and do so in practical ways.

SESSION 11

SOCIAL JUSTICE

"The moment the idea is admitted into society that property is not as sacred as the laws of God, and that there is not a force of law and public justice to protect it, anarchy and tyranny commence. If 'Thou shalt not covet' and 'Thou shalt not steal' were not commandments of Heaven, they must be made inviolable precepts in every society before it can be civilized or made free."

— John Adams

11 SESSION

SOCIAL JUSTICE

INTRODUCTION

Many Christians today are sympathetic to the modern Social Justice movement. True social justice — taking care of the most vulnerable and neediest among us — is indeed an important concern for every Christian. However, secularists have hijacked the traditional social justice concern for the poor and used it to call for things that God never intended and which He even opposes. In our desire to care for the less fortunate, we have become unwitting tools of a Progressive big government agenda seeking to fundamentally redefine the role of the Family, the Church, and Civil Government.

The Scripture certainly is not silent on the topic of social justice. God unequivocally commands us to care for the poor and needy. But for us to do this in the manner stipulated by the Bible looks very different than what many people now believe. Thus, to conform to the Scriptural principles defining the implementation of true social justice will require a major paradigm shift for many well-meaning social justice activists today.

In this session, you will learn:

- What the Bible says about caring for the poor
- The role of government in caring for the needy
- How God defines social justice
- How Christians should determine voting priorities when considering social justice issues
- The unBiblical premise undergirding the modern global warming debate

DISCUSSION QUESTIONS BEFORE WATCHING THE VIDEO

1. Which is more important: caring for the planet or ending abortion? Give a Biblical basis for your answer.
2. Why does it seem that the secular world is more concerned about social justice than the church is?
3. Do our current laws help the poor or harm them? Why?

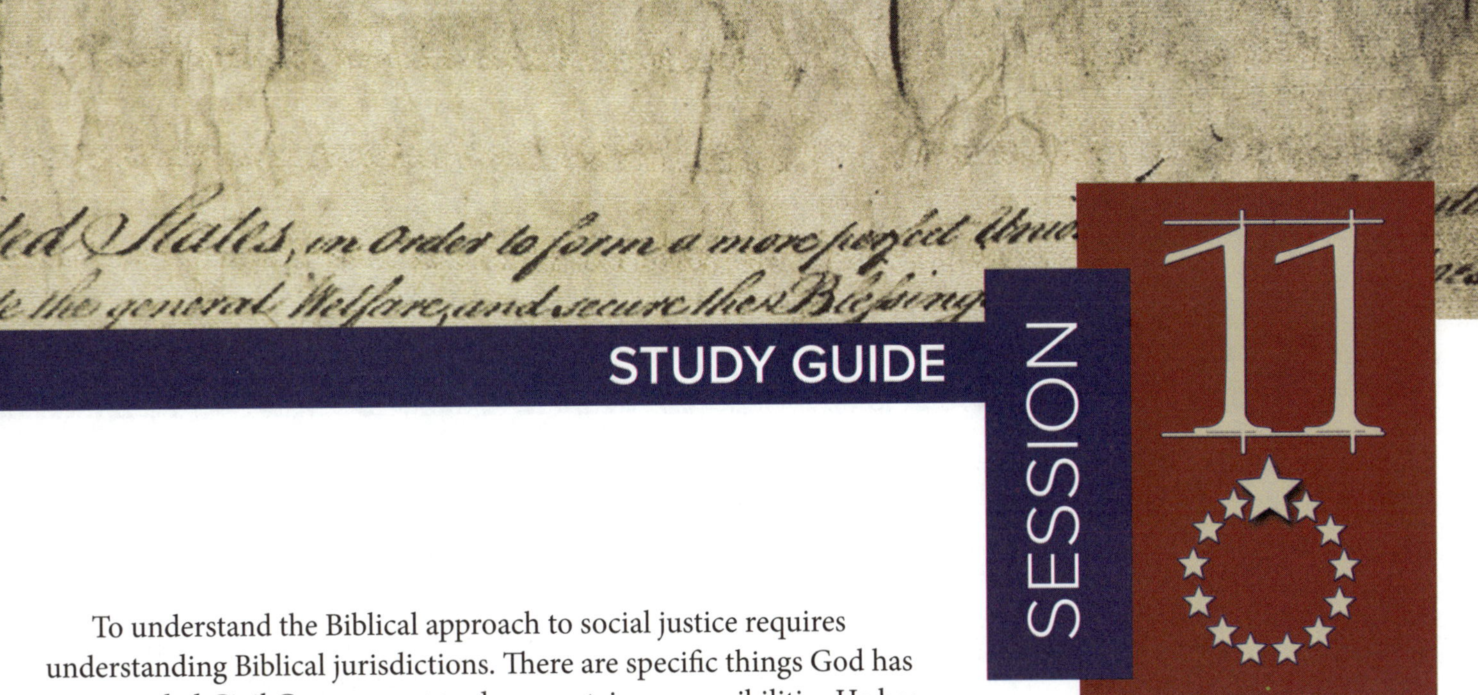

To understand the Biblical approach to social justice requires understanding Biblical jurisdictions. There are specific things God has commanded Civil Government to do — certain responsibilities He has commanded it to perform. So, too, with the Family, the Church, and the Individual (see Lesson #3 for more on this).

The modern view of social justice is that government should be the primary instrument for meeting the needs of the poor. In fact, nearly sixty percent of Americans believe that dealing with the poor should be a top priority of the president and Congress; they are even willing to pay higher taxes to help ensure that this occurs.

JURISDICTION
The limits of authority or power, and the sphere in which it may be exercised.

The genuine poor do need to be helped, and scores of Bible verses address how to meet their needs. But significantly, nearly all of these verses are directed at individuals and the church; government is not charged with meeting their material needs.

In fact, history and current statistics both unequivocally demonstrate that government is one of the most inefficient and ineffective delivery systems for aid to the poor. This reality is unequivocally affirmed by the American Institute of Philanthropy (AIP), also known as Charity Watch (CW). CW rates various organizations by calculating the percentage of donated income that actually makes it to the intended target, and according to CW, a charity's effectiveness is "acceptable" if 60 percent of what it collects reaches its intended mission. Donors should avoid contributing to organizations where less than 60 percent of contributed funds reach the designated target.

So what percentage of every dollar collected by the government for the benefit of the poor actually reaches them? A dismal 30 percent. The U. S. government is quite possibly the nation's most inefficient mechanism for meeting the needs of the poor. No reasonable contributor would fund an organization where only 30 cents out of each dollar reached its target, but

11 SESSION

STUDY GUIDE

many today not only tolerate such malfeasance but even encourage more government spending to fight poverty. Why? — Just to see 70 percent of each additional dollar wasted?

Furthermore, the more government increases its role with the poor, the more it harms the Church. An international study in 33 nations demonstrates that when government spending on the poor rises, church attendance falls. Government is assuming the role of God and is trying to meet needs that God intended to be met through personal human contact from individuals and the church, not impersonal governmental contact.

SOCIALISM
Any of various economic and political theories advocating collective or governmental ownership and administration of the means of production and distribution of goods

So, the government's clamor that it needs to do more to take care of the poor is actually an excuse for increasing taxes, expanding power, and promoting a more socialistic form of government.

Question #1: Jesus told us to take care of the poor. So shouldn't that be an issue when we vote?

The only responsibility God gives government in regard to the poor is to maintain their rights and ensure they get justice whenever they utilize the civil process:

> *"You shall not show partiality to a poor man in his dispute....You shall not pervert the judgment of your poor in his dispute."*
>
> — Exodus 23:3-6

It is not in the jurisdiction of Civil Government to meet the material needs of the poor. But the Bible is clear about who does have that responsibility — Individuals, the Church, and the Family:

> *"Is this not the fast that I have chosen: to loosen the bonds of wickedness, to undo the heavy burdens, to let the oppressed go free, and that you break every yoke? Is it not to share **your** bread with the hungry, and that **you** bring to **your** house the poor who are cast out; when **you** see the naked, that **you** cover him...?"*
>
> — Isaiah 58:6-7

In The Message version, this passage states:

> ***"This is the kind of fast day I'm after: to break the chains of injustice, get rid of exploitation in the workplace, free the oppressed, cancel debts. What I'm interested in seeing you do is: sharing your food with the hungry, inviting the homeless poor into your homes, putting clothes on the shivering ill-clad, being available to your own families."***
>
> — Isaiah 58:6-7 (The Message)

God was speaking to His people in this Scripture, not to Civil Government. The same is true with other noted Biblical passages on this subject:

> ***When you happen on someone who's in trouble or needs help among your people with whom you live in this land that God gave you, don't look the other way pretending you don't see him — don't keep a tight grip on your purse. No. Look at him; open your purse; lend whatever and as much as he needs... Give freely and spontaneously. Don't have a stingy heart. The way you handle matters like this triggers God's blessing in everything you do — all your work and ventures. There are always going to be poor and needy people among you. So I command you: Always be generous; open purse and hands; give to your neighbors in trouble — your poor and hurting neighbors.***
>
> — Deuteronomy 15:7-8, 10-11 (The Message)

Again, this is a directive to God's people, not to Civil Government.

Jesus likewise declared:

> ***"Then the King will say to those on His right hand, 'Come, you blessed of My Father, inherit the kingdom prepared for you from the foundation of the world: for I was hungry and you gave Me food; I was thirsty and you gave Me drink; I was a stranger and you took Me in; I was naked and you clothed Me; I was sick and you visited Me; I was in prison and you came to Me.....inasmuch as you did it to one of the least of these My brethren, you did it to Me.'"***
>
> — Matthew 25:34-36

"You shall not show partiality to a poor man in his dispute...You shall not pervert the judgment of your poor in his dispute."
— Exodus 23:3-6

Who did Jesus instruct to provide relief to the hungry, the thirsty, the needy, and the prisoner? Was it Civil Government? No. He told His disciples — His followers.

11 SESSION STUDY GUIDE

This pattern is followed with dozens of other Scriptures in the Bible addressing the subject of taking care of the poor, and this is the model followed by the Founding Fathers: Civil Government did not provide charity; the people did. As George Washington affirmed:

> Let your heart feel for the afflictions and distresses of every one, and let your hand give in proportion to your purse, remembering always the estimation of the widow's mite, but that it is not every one who asketh that deserveth charity; all, however, are worthy of the inquiry, or the deserving may suffer.

"Therefore God also gave them up to uncleanness, in the lusts of their hearts, to dishonor their bodies among themselves, who exchanged the truth of God for the lie, and worshiped and served the creature rather than the Creator, who is blessed forever. Amen."
— Romans 1:24-25

There is simply no Biblical model for a Civil Government welfare system. Furthermore, while God made sure that there would be provision for the poor, He also mandated that unless they were physically unable to do so, the poor were required to do some work to receive the needed help. For example, as part of providing for the poor, God told the farmers and landowners:

> ***"When you reap the harvest of your land, you shall not wholly reap the corners of your field, nor shall you gather the gleanings of your harvest. And you shall not glean your vineyard, nor shall you gather every grape of your vineyard; you shall leave them for the poor and the stranger: I am the Lord your God."***
>
> — Leviticus 19:9-10

Here, God again made provision for taking care of the poor. But notice, the poor had to harvest the corners of the field to get the wheat, and to also gather the grapes — they had to do some work to get their needs met. The Bible explicitly directs that if someone does not work, then he is not to be given free welfare or food (II Thessalonian 3:10) — except in the very rare cases when someone was physically unable to work — paralyzed, elderly, too young, and so forth (James 1:27, 1 Timothy 5:3-10, etc.).

> ***I am for doing good to the poor, but... I think the best way of doing good to the poor, is not making them easy in poverty, but leading or driving them out of it.***
>
> — Benjamin Franklin

Poverty should be a temporary condition for any individual, not a perpetual one — which is what it often becomes when Civil Government wrongly usurps that responsibility away from the other institutions.

Question #2: As Christians, shouldn't we be fighting global warming?

The real question concerning global warming is not whether or not it occurs, but whether it is anthropogenic — that is, whether it is caused by human activities, or is the result of causes outside of man's direct control, such as sun-spot cycles, or meteorological cyclical warming and cooling periods that historically have often lasted decades, sometimes even centuries.

Genesis 1-3 teaches us that God created everything that exists — and He created it in an ascending order of importance, moving from the inanimate to the animate. The capstone of His creation was man, and He gave man dominion over the planet and everything on it (Genesis 1:26-28). Man wasn't created to serve the planet, but rather the planet to serve man.

The supporters of global warming legislation say that we need to restrict our lives so that we can save (i.e., serve) the planet. They have reversed God's order — they have placed the creation above the Creator. As evidenced by the numerous debates in Congress, global warming leaders are willing to sacrifice or regulate almost anything to save the planet, but very few things to save human life. Ironically, in the political realm the strongest advocates of environmentalism, global warming, and endangered species measures are generally the most rabid supporters of abortion — of taking and not protecting innocent human life. They place every other issue above man and want man to be subservient to the planet.

Interestingly, the "science" on these issues continues to change, and change rapidly. What was once a major concern among scientists no longer is, for the measurements indicate not only that the crisis has largely passed but even that the trend is moving in the opposite direction. It is political figures, not scientists, who largely have kept these issues alive and at the forefront of American thinking, urging additional government spending and expansion of government powers to intervene and save the planet from man.

God gave man dominion over the earth, including all inanimate things, placing those resources at man's disposal, not vice versa. Efforts to reverse that order are direct affronts to the plan of God for man and nature.

> *"Therefore God also gave them up to uncleanness, in the lusts of their hearts, to dishonor their bodies among themselves, who exchanged the truth of God for the lie, and worshiped and served the creature rather than the Creator, Who is blessed forever. Amen."*
>
> — Romans 1:24-25

Question #3: There's a lot more in the Bible besides abortion and marriage. Why do people get stuck on these issues?

In the political realm, many modern social justice advocates avow that they don't want to become "one-issue voters" — that they don't want to become "fixated" on narrow things like abortion and marriage when there are so many other important issues to also consider. But such objections actually serve to take Christians' focus off of and to dilute support for undeniably crucial issues such as abortion, marriage, the rights of religious conscience, and the public acknowledgement of God.

In any political cycle, several dozen issues always arise, ranging from taxation to the military, from education to debt, from abortion to immigration, and healthcare to foreign affairs. Every one of these issues is important — and every one of them is addressed in the Bible. When God organized His nation of Israel, He delivered to them a comprehensive code containing 613 laws — laws that also address the issues we deal with today. But God made it abundantly clear that some issues were more important to Him than others, for from those 613 laws, God selected His "Top Ten," or what we call the Ten Commandments. This is God's prioritization of those issues most significant to Him.

God's Top Ten includes things such as a prohibition against shedding innocent blood (which is what occurs with abortion); a mandate to keep the marriage bed as He originally designed it (which requires that sexual relations be between only a man and a woman in a lifelong union; so homosexual marriage and other sexual arrangements and behaviors are thus addressed here); and God's Top Ten also commands us to secure the open and public acknowledgment of Him (of which the rights of religious conscience is an implicit part). These are among the most important issues to God, but things such as social justice, environmental care, taxation, immigration, and many other issues did NOT make His Top Ten.

These three high-ranking issues, selected and emphasized by God Himself, should therefore be at the forefront of a Christian's decision-making when voting. It is only after you have determined that a candidate is acceptable on these three non-negotiables that you should extend your consideration to include other issues, such as economics, foreign policy, taxes, or health care. To do otherwise is to elevate an issue above where God Himself placed it and to usurp His authority and that of His word, placing our will and opinion above His.

> ***"Then the Lord said to Moses, 'Write these words, for according to the tenor of these words I have made a covenant with you and with Israel."***
>
> — Exodus 34:27

 ADDITIONAL READING/VIEWING/LISTENING

- *Eight Steps to Thinking Biblically* by David Barton
- *Developing a Biblical Worldview* by David Barton
- *Science, the Bible, and Global Warming* by David Barton
- *The Principles of Limited Government* by David Barton
- *The Founders' Bible* by David Barton

11 SESSION

STUDY GUIDE

★ DISCUSSION QUESTIONS AFTER WATCHING THE VIDEO

1. How does God command the poor to be cared for?

Christians are commanded to care for the poor out of our own resources. Nowhere does Scripture say that government is to take our resources and use them for charity. We are told to open our own hearts and homes to aid the needy. Caring for the poor is not the role of Civil Government; it is the role of Individuals, the Family, and the Church.

2. Isn't it a big deal to God how we treat the earth?

How we treat each other is a much bigger deal to God than how we treat the earth. Scripture talks much more about how we interact with our fellow humans than it does about how we interact with the earth or anything else. God gave us the earth and told us to subdue and take dominion over it. While we should be good stewards, anything that places a priority on the earth above man and man's ability to harness the earth is unBiblical.

3. What issues does God want Christians to be most concerned about?

God's priorities for any people or society are reflected in the Ten Commandments. The issues in those Commandments that most readily relate to American public policy issues today include those of the public acknowledgment and honoring of God (which involves protecting the rights of religious conscience), protecting innocent human life (abortion, euthanasia, assisted suicide, and the like), and preserving sexuality exclusively within God-ordained and God-defined marriage. Christians should vote for leaders who prioritize these issues among their highest concerns. To place others issues higher than these is to exalt our will above His.

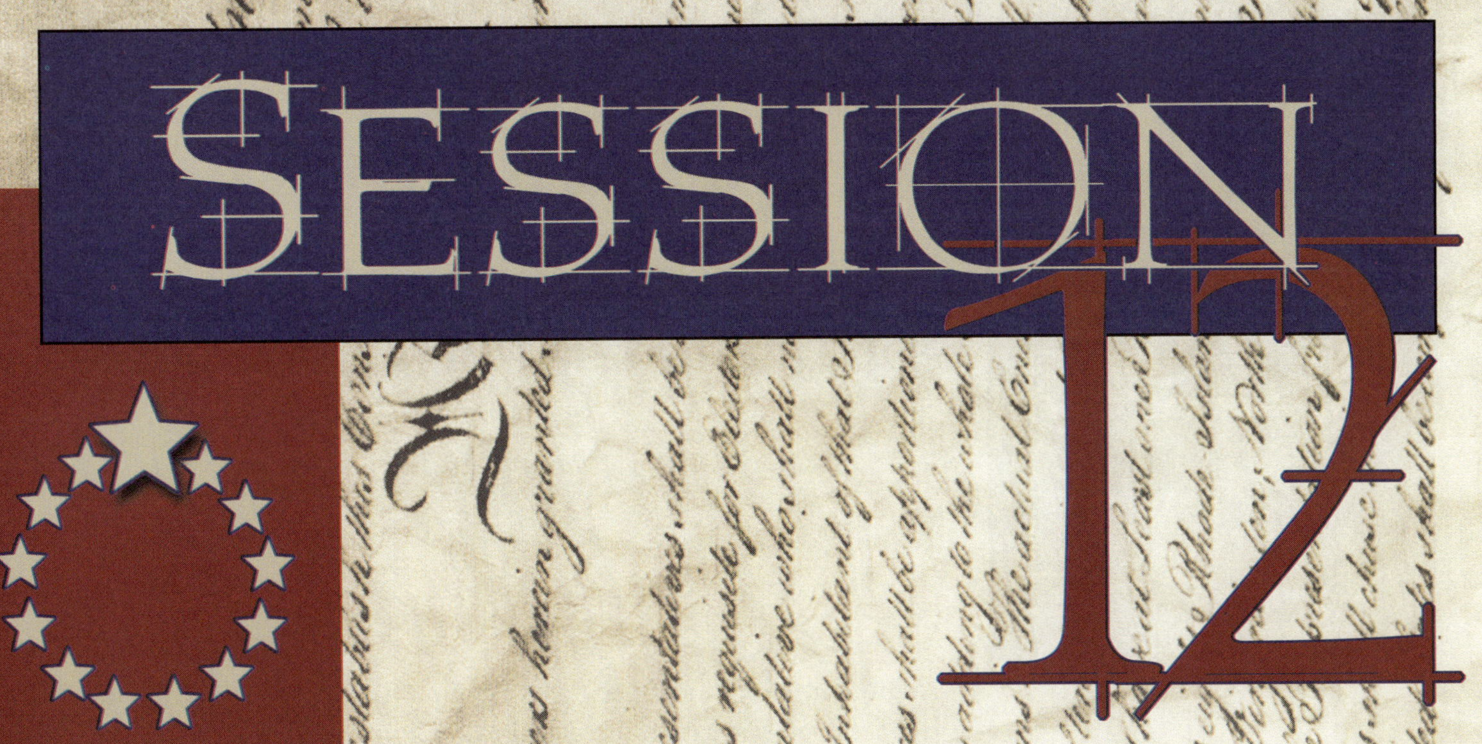

POLITICS IN THE PULPIT

"In the language of Holy Writ, there is a time for all things, a time to preach and a time to pray, but those times have passed away. There is a time to fight — and that time has now come!"

— Rev. John Peter Gabriel Muhlenberg
Sermon at Woodstock
Virginia, January 21, 1776

12 SESSION

POLITICS IN THE PULPIT

INTRODUCTION

Many Christians today separate the pulpit from politics, viewing them as two completely separate and even incompatible spheres. But this was not the position of early American Christians, including in the Founding Era. In fact, both American and British leaders agreed that colonial ministers were a driving force behind American Independence. Yet far more important than this historical precedent is the fact that the separation of politics from the pulpit is not supported by the Scriptures.

Today's failure to understand why politics actually can and should be addressed from the pulpit is largely rooted in a misunderstanding of what politics actually is. According to Founding Father Noah Webster, who penned America's first dictionary, "Politics" is:

> The science of government; that part of ethics which consists in the regulation and government of a nation or state for the preservation of its safety, peace, and prosperity... and the protection of its citizens in their rights, with the preservation and improvement of their morals.

The modern definition is not much different, being "the activities associated with the governance of a country or other area, especially the debate or conflict among individuals or parties having or hoping to achieve power."

It will be very hard for any Christian to assert that the Bible does not address either the ethics that are to regulate a nation, or the measures involved with the preservation and improvement of its morals. And it is equally difficult to argue that Christians should not be involved in the debates associated with the formation of such policies. All of this is central to politics, and discussions about such things are certainly a point of frequent emphasis throughout the Bible.

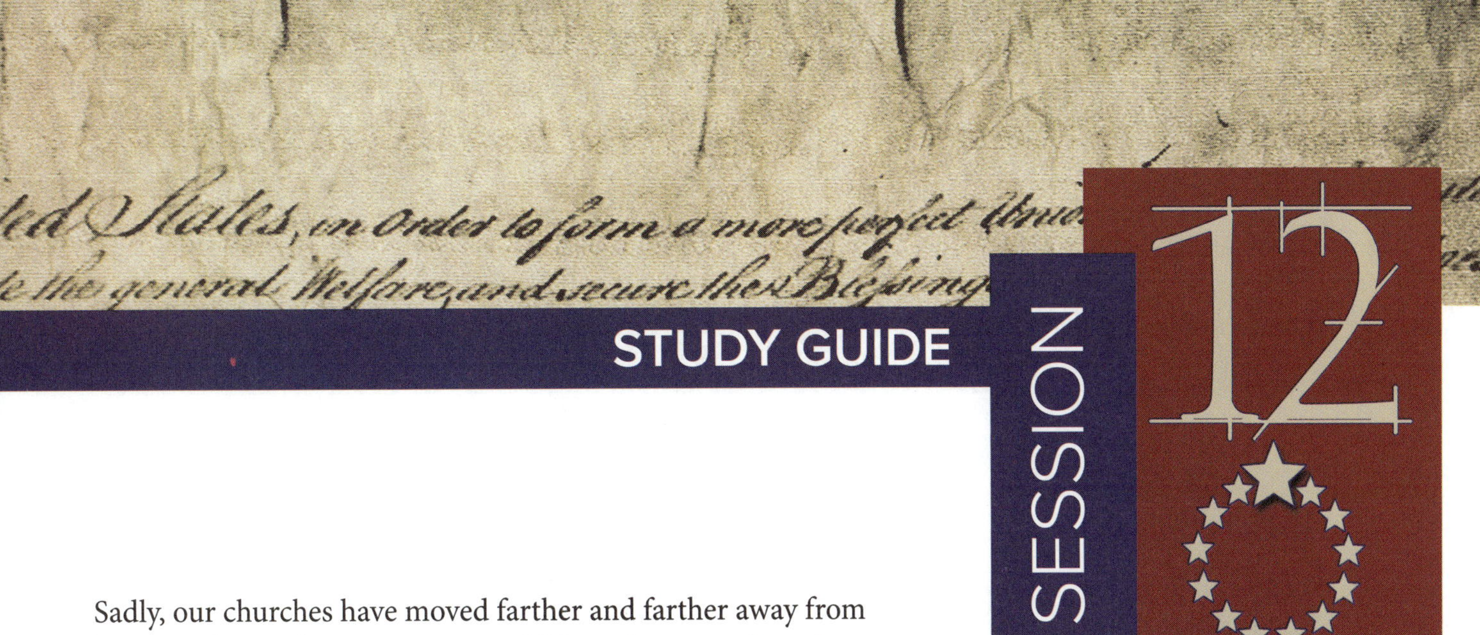

Sadly, our churches have moved farther and farther away from applying God's Word to every aspect of life, and as a result we have witnessed the decline of the church's relevance in our culture today. It's time for our churches and pastors to reassume the vital role in society that the Scripture calls them to, addressing the ethics, morals, and public policies of our communities, states, and nation, and entering into and shaping the debate on these important issues.

In this lesson, you will learn:

- The impact of colonial pastors on the American Revolution
- Numerous Biblical examples of God's ministers directly addressing public policies
- The constitutional right of pastors to speak on any issue
- The IRS myth that keeps many pastors silent on politics
- What Jesus had to say about politics
- The balance between keeping unity in the church and addressing public policy issues

DISCUSSION QUESTIONS BEFORE WATCHING THE VIDEO

1. Shouldn't the church be a refuge from things like politics?
2. How can a pastor minister effectively to everyone if he takes sides in politics?
3. Does the Bible address any of the political issues of our day?

British leaders, believing that American preachers were responsible for American Independence, dubbed those early preachers the "Black Regiment" (a reference to the black clerical robes that ministers wore in that day). Significantly, every right set forth in the 1776 Declaration of Independence had been preached from the American pulpit by 1763; the Declaration therefore embodied the teachings of the pulpit.

12 SESSION STUDY GUIDE

One of the many examples illustrating the influence of pastors and their sermons in shaping American thinking is evident in 1772, when the Sons of Liberty (the leaders among the American patriots) reprinted key sermons of the Rev. John Wise (1652-1725). Significantly, the Rev. Wise is considered by modern historians as one of the six greatest intellectual forces who most directly "contributed to the rise of political liberty" in America. (Of the remaining five, three — the Rev. Thomas Hooker, the Rev. Roger Williams, and the Rev. Jonathan Mayhew — were also ministers. The two non-ministers were Benjamin Franklin and Richard Bland.)

As early as 1687, the Rev. Wise was already teaching that "taxation without representation is tyranny," that the "consent of the governed" was the foundation of government, and that all men were created equal. In 1926, President Calvin Coolidge delivered a speech on the 150th anniversary of the Declaration of Independence, acknowledging, "These thoughts [in the Declaration] can very largely be traced back to what John Wise was writing."

READ MORE

- *The Chaplains and Clergy of the Revolution* by J. T. Headley
- *The Pulpit of the American Revolution* by John Wingate Thornton

(These are available for free reading and pdf download at Books.Google.com.)

Considering the common practice of pastors addressing the issues of the day, it is not surprising that John Adams affirmed that the "the pulpits have thundered," adding that "the clergy of every denomination, [including] the Episcopalian, thunder and lightning every Sabbath." He also identified the Rev. Dr. Mayhew and the Rev. Dr. Cooper as two of the "characters . . . most conspicuous, the most ardent, and influential" in "an awakening and a revival of American principles and feelings . . . in 1775."

Had it not been for the substantial influence and leadership of the American pulpit, America might never have become a free and independent nation.

STUDY GUIDE

SESSION 12

Question #1: Preachers were definitely involved in the American Revolution, but that was before the First Amendment became part of the Constitution. So aren't pastors to stay out of politics today?

Before the Constitution was adopted, pastors in the Revolution definitely were involved in numerous public spheres, including as:

- military soldiers, officers, and chaplains
- legislators and statesmen
- authors of state constitutions

The First Amendment made no change in these practices. In fact, the Bill of Rights (which contains the First Amendment) is signed by only two individuals: John Adams, president of the U. S. Senate and Vice President of the United States, and Frederick Augustus Muhlenberg, Speaker of the U. S. House of Representatives. Significantly, Muhlenberg was a minister of the Gospel, as were several members of that first federal Congress, including the Revs. John Peter Gabriel Muhlenberg (brother of the Speaker), Abiel Foster, Benjamin Contee, Abraham Baldwin, and Paine Wingate.

> ***Congress shall make no law respecting an establishment of religion, or prohibiting the free exercise thereof; or abridging the freedom of speech, or of the press; or the right of the people peaceably to assemble, and to petition the Government for a redress of grievances.***
>
> — First Amendment of the Constitution

As noted in Lesson #3, the purpose of the First Amendment was not to secularize government or reduce the influence of pastors or churches but rather was to ensure that the government would not interfere with or limit these positive forces. One of the evidences of this fact is that multiple of the Founding Fathers openly supported the right of ministers to serve in public office.

12 SESSION

STUDY GUIDE

Consider Thomas Jefferson as an example. Throughout the time when there had been government-established denominations in America, Jefferson opposed clergymen serving in office. But once all denominations were placed on the same equal footing, Jefferson supported the right of clergymen to be elected, declaring:

> I observe however in the same scheme of a [Virginia] constitution an abridgment of the right of being elected which...I do not approve. It is the incapacitation of a clergyman from being elected...The clergy here seem to have relinquished all pretension to privilege and to stand on a footing with lawyers, physicians &c. They ought therefore to possess the same rights.

Virginia did remove that "incapacitation" against ministers. And when Georgia similarly attempted to prevent clergymen from being elected to office, signer of the Declaration John Witherspoon likewise strongly objected, declaring:

> "Before any man among us was ordained a minister, was he not a citizen of the United States, and if being in Georgia, a citizen of the state of Georgia? Had he not then a right to be elected a member of the assembly, if qualified in point of property?"

Georgia, too, removed its prohibition against clergymen serving in office.

In short, clergymen, churches, and the pulpit have the same free speech protection as other citizens, institutions, and corporations, and they have every right — and even every duty — to be involved in shaping both the public debate and the public policy resulting from it.

> ***"The priest's lips should keep knowledge, and they [the people] should seek the law at his mouth."***
>
> — Malachi 2:7

Question #2: Shouldn't pastors keep their focus on the church and not on politics?

As Lesson #1 affirmed, the Bible does not establish an "either-or" scenario requiring Christians to choose between church and public policy issues. Rather, the Bible teaches that Christians have clear duties in both areas. Today we too often hold the wrong view: that there is an unbridgeable chasm between church and public policy. But God and His Word do not take that position. While God does establish an institutional separation between Church and Civil Government (see Lesson #3), He does not exclude His presence or His policies from either. In fact, three times in Romans 13:3-6, God says that those in Civil Government are His "ministers" — the same word He uses to describe those in the pulpit.

Additionally, in Hebrews 11 (our "Faith Hall of Fame" wherein the great heroes of our faith are held up to us as examples), every hero listed in verses 22-34 was involved in Civil Government. Why would God hold such individuals up to us as examples to inspire us if He thought it was wrong for His people to be involved in the civil arena?

In fact, consider how often God sent His ministers either directly to confront civil leaders or to publicly expose their wicked policies:

- Elijah confronted King Ahab and Queen Jezebel over issues such as their unjust use of eminent domain and religious persecution (I Kings 21:1-24, I Kings 18:18)
- Eliezer and Jehu confronted King Jehoshaphat over his blunders in foreign relations and ill-advised foreign alliances (II Chronicles 19:1-2, II Chronicles 20:35-37)
- Isaiah confronted King Hezekiah over national security failures and issues related to the treasury (II Chronicles 32:27-31, II Kings 20:12-19)
- Nathan confronted David over his wicked moral policies and practices (II Samuel 12)

12 SESSION

STUDY GUIDE

- God's prophet Gad confronted David over his wrong-headed public policies that stemmed from his own pride and arrogance (II Samuel 24)
- Azariah (along with eighty other priests) confronted King Uzziah for usurping religious practices through an improper expansion of government powers (II Chronicles 26:16-21)
- Samuel confronted King Saul over not fulfilling his assigned responsibilities (I Samuel 13:1-14, I Samuel 15)
- Micaiah regularly confronted King Ahab over his wicked public policies (I Kings 22:7-18)
- Daniel confronted Nebuchadnezzar over his pride and arrogance (Daniel 4:1-27) and Belshazzar over his moral debauchery (Daniel 5:17-28)
- Jeremiah confronted King Zedekiah over numerous of his wicked public policies (Jeremiah 34)
- John the Baptist confronted civil leaders for their hypocrisy (Matthew 3:7) and King Herod over his divorce and marriage practices (Luke 13:32, Matthew 23:23, 27, 33)

There are numerous other examples, and there is no Biblical model wherein God requires that His ministers remain silent about civil leaders or public policy issues. But His spiritual leaders not only called out bad civil leaders and confronted bad policy, they also were frequently involved in constructing good policies and providing sound civil guidance. For example:

- King Joash pursued good policies as long as the priest Jehoiada was providing him counsel, but when King Joash no longer had that righteous input, his policies became wicked (II Chronicles 24:1-2, 15-19)
- Nathan provided guidance to David on architectural issues (II Samuel 7:1-13)

- Elisha provided the King of Israel counsel regarding military intelligence and military policy issues (II Kings 6)
- Ezra gave strong counsel on marriage policy (Ezra 9-10 passim), and Governor Nehemiah implemented that counsel into public policy (Nehemiah 8:1-6, 13:23-27)
- Paul provided civil leaders with guidance during times of impending disaster and natural calamity (Acts 27:9-12)
- Jeremiah provided military guidance to King Zedekiah (Jeremiah 21:1-10)
- Isaiah gave King Hezekiah guidance on national security issues and foreign policy (Isaiah 37)

The Bible is loaded — and almost overflowing — with accounts of God's ministers not only speaking into the civil arena but also speaking directly to (and about) civil leaders.

Question #3: Did Jesus spend any time talking about government or public policy in His time?

Jesus specifically called out King Herod (Luke 13:31-32) as well as other civil leaders (Matthew 23). And numerous of His teachings directly addressed things that have definitely become public policy issues today — such as the definition of marriage, and the wrongness of no-fault divorce (Matthew 19), economic practices (Luke 19), labor relations (Matthew 20), and criminal justice rights (John 8). (For an in-depth explanation of Jesus' teachings on these subjects, see *The Founders' Bible* by David Barton.) Jesus spoke about many of these issues before they became political, and the Church is not relieved from addressing them simply because the government has intruded into areas that once were (and still remain) topics of moral and Biblical emphasis (such as marriage, divorce, homosexuality, education, the rights of conscience, debt, and numerous others).

12 SESSION
STUDY GUIDE

The Church's position should be: if it's in the Bible, then we're going to talk about it in the pulpit, regardless of whether or not it is considered a political issue today. Pastors should expound the practical application of the Word of God to every aspect of daily life, and a pastor or church should never avoid speaking out for fear of the Internal Revenue Service (IRS). A church's tax-exemption comes from the Constitution, not from any government regulatory agency. (For more information about this, go to SpeakUpMovement.org.)

Question #4: My church is full of people with differing political views. Should I be concerned that introducing politics into the pulpit will breed disunity in the church?

First, remember that by definition, "politics" is merely the discussion over public policy issues that relate to morals, ethics, and the operation of government. If the Bible addresses these issues, then so must the Church, regardless of the consequences.

Second, it is a mistake to place a supposed "unity" above the proclamation of truth. Jesus always delivered the truth, and it definitely did not always produce unity.

> ***"Do you suppose that I came to give peace on earth? I tell you, not at all, but rather division. For from now on five in one house will be divided: three against two, and two against three."***
>
> — Luke 12:51-52

Even many of the most religious folks were often offended by what He said:

> ***Later His disciples came and told him, "Did you know how upset the Pharisees were when they heard what you said?" Jesus shrugged it off. "Every tree that wasn't planted by my Father in heaven will be pulled up by its roots. Forget them. They are blind men leading blind men. When a blind man leads a blind man, they both end up in the ditch."***
>
> — Matthew 15:12-14 The Message version

In fact, many of His own disciples rejected what Jesus said:

> ***Therefore many of His disciples, when they heard this, said, "This is a hard saying; who can understand it?" When Jesus knew in Himself that His disciples complained about this, He said to them, "Does this offend you? ... From that time many of His disciples went back and walked with Him no more. Then Jesus said to the twelve, "Do you also want to go away?" But Simon Peter answered Him, "Lord, to whom shall we go? You have the words of eternal life."***
>
> — John 6:60-61, 66-69; NKJV

Jesus' ministry was not about increasing His numbers through an absence of conflict. Rather, his mission was to hold up God's Word and standards of righteousness, regardless of the response it received. It is always more important to get people to think Biblically than it is to have a false unity created by remaining silent on controversial issues on which the Bible takes a clear stand.

ADDITIONAL READING/VIEWING/LISTENING

- *The Role of Pastors & Christians in Civil Government* by David Barton
- *Biblical Principles and the Political Process* by David Barton
- *The Genesis Journeys* by Rabbi Daniel Lapin

DISCUSSION QUESTIONS AFTER WATCHING THE VIDEO

1. What effect has the church's reluctance to address politics had on society?

- A decreasing sense of Christian civic stewardship and responsibility
- An absence of salt and light, which always leads to increased sin and corruption, including in the political arena
- Increasing numbers and types of unBiblical and unrighteous policies
- Loss of God-given inalienable rights and freedoms, including the right to openly and publicly acknowledge God according to the dictates of conscience
- An increasing irrelevance of the church in society and the culture

2. How can I encourage my pastor to address political issues?

Show your pastor the numerous verses and Biblical examples where God's ministers addressed public policy issues. Also introduce your pastor to the many examples and sermons from American history showing that for over three centuries, God's ministers in America did the same. (Much additional information on the American examples is available at NationalBlackRobeRegiment.com, and scores of early American sermons are posted in their entirety at WallBuilders.com.)

3. How should we keep politics from breeding disunity?

So long as teaching Biblical truth is your objective, there will be disunity for there will always be those, including in the Christian community, who will dislike and will be offended by Biblical teachings. Conflict is certainly not your objective, but don't be surprised when it occurs. And because conflict can sometimes be caused by judgmental and arrogant attitudes rather than just content, it's important for Christians to keep a spirit of grace and humility when discussing the Bible's hard positions, including those regarding specific public policies. Many people will be willing to entertain and consider a position very different to their own if it is presented in a humble and respectful way.

SESSION 13

CHRISTIANS IN THE CIVIL ARENA

"Providence has given to our people the choice of their rulers, and it is the duty, as well as the privilege and interest of our Christian nation, to select and prefer Christians for their rulers."

— John Jay
Original Chief Justice of the U. S. Supreme Court
author of *The Federalist Papers*

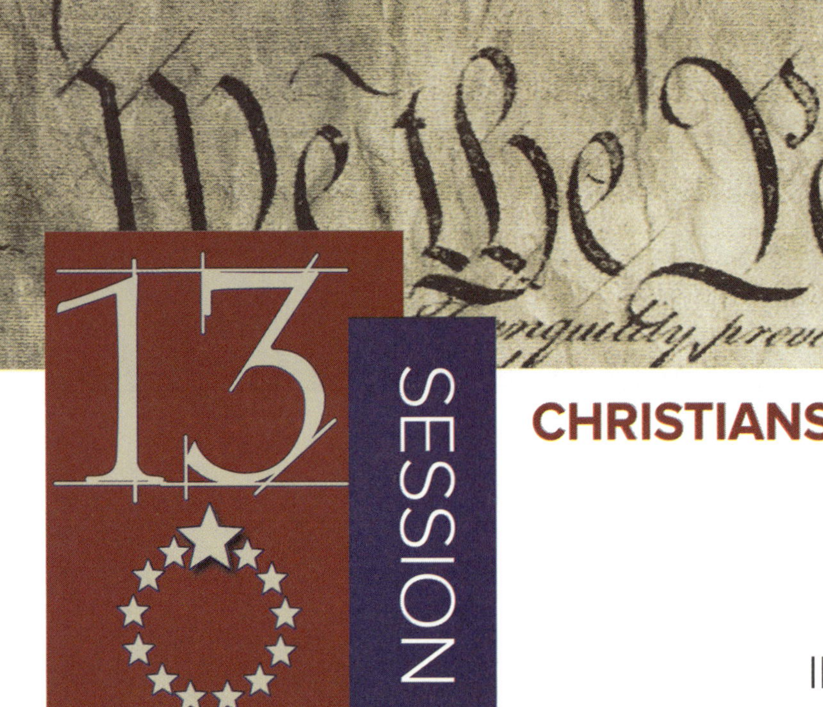

CHRISTIANS IN THE CIVIL ARENA

INTRODUCTION

Political involvement has become a tricky subject for Christians today. Is it appropriate to be involved in politics as a Christian? And if you are involved, does it really do any good? And just how much do you have to know about politics and the political process to be effective?

The good news is that it doesn't take a degree in political science to make a difference. Contrary to popular perception, the political process is not that complicated, and the simple principles of God's Word are fully applicable to it. All it takes is a willingness to get involved.

It's time for Christians to return to the historical and Biblical understanding of a Christian's active role in politics. Our Founding Fathers understood that Christians have a responsibility to be involved in every area of life, including the political sphere; and as the salt and light of society (Matthew 5:13-14), we play an indispensable role in the direction of our nation — a direction that will be for good if we choose to be involved or for evil if we refuse to engage. Sadly, too many Christians prefer to be only light rather than salt: light is passive but salt is active — that is, light is quiet and often still and motionless, but salt can definitely burn and sting when applied to infected and putrefying areas (which is often what is found in the public governmental sphere).

> ***"You are the salt of the earth; but if the salt loses its flavor, how shall it be seasoned? It is then good for nothing but to be thrown out and trampled underfoot by men. You are the light of the world. A city that is set on a hill cannot be hidden."***
>
> — Matthew 5:13-14 (NKJV)

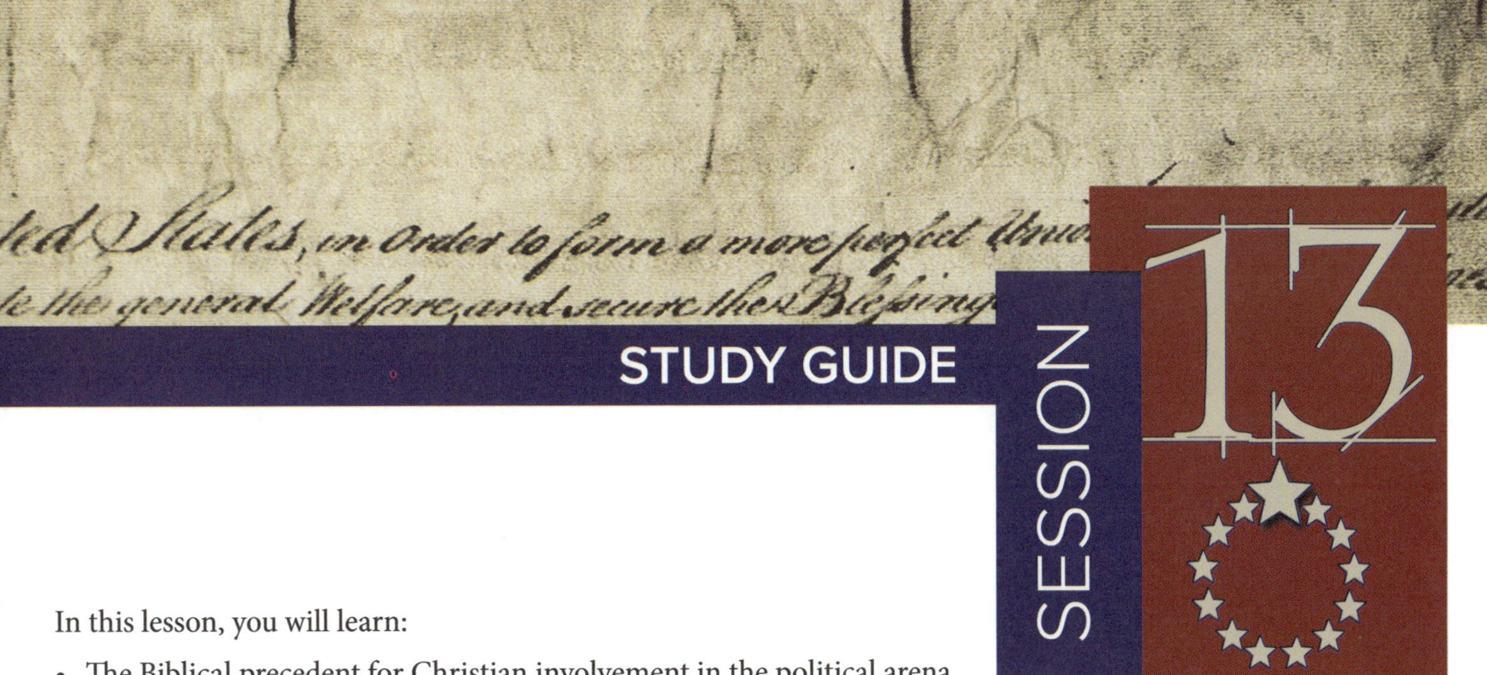

In this lesson, you will learn:

- The Biblical precedent for Christian involvement in the political arena
- How a proper understanding of the issue of preserving unborn life can help you analyze candidates on all other issues
- The impact of Christian voter turnout
- How to get reliable information about candidates
- What occurs when Christians don't vote their values

 DISCUSSION QUESTIONS BEFORE WATCHING THE VIDEO

1. Is it more important to witness than to be involved in politics?
2. Does Scripture actually command us to vote, or is it up to us?
3. Does voting our values mean we can't consider things like the economy?

As noted in the Lesson #12, many of the heroes listed in the Hebrews 11 "Faith Hall of Fame" were directly involved in civil government, and God specifically says that those who serve in that arena are "God's ministers."

> *"For he is God's **minister** to you for good. But if you do evil, be afraid; for he does not bear the sword in vain; for he is God's **minister**, an avenger to execute wrath on him who practices evil. Therefore you must be subject, not only because of wrath but also for conscience' sake. For because of this you also pay taxes, for they are God's **ministers** attending continually to this very thing."*
>
> — Romans 13:4-6

13 SESSION

STUDY GUIDE

Significantly, God does not distinguish between the spiritual and the secular, as we often do today. He holds that His principles apply to ***every*** aspect of life, and He does not exempt any arena simply because we somehow consider it to be "unspiritual." God designed ***everything*** to be operated under His principles, and that to do so is for our own benefit and good.

One indication of the positive viewpoint that the Lord holds toward Civil Government is found in Luke 19. In that passage, the Master calls His servants together and gives them all a mina — a trust — a stewardship. The Master departs and then later returns to take account of their service. One servant had taken the mina and turned it into ten; another had turned his into five; and another had taken his trust and not used it at all. The one who refused to get involved with what the Master had entrusted him was the one who got in trouble, but notice the reward for the other two. To the first, the Master said, "Well done good and faithful servant; I will make you a ruler over ten cities." To the second he said, "Well done, I will make you a ruler over five cities."

Notice the reward of the Master for their faithful stewardship: he placed them into Civil Government! Today, most Christians would not think of this as being a reward from the Master, so perhaps it is time to rethink our beliefs about Civil Government based on what the Bible says.

> *"And He said to him, 'Well done, good servant. Because you were faithful in a very little, have authority over ten cities.' And the second came, saying, 'Master, your mina has earned five minas.' Likewise He said to him, 'You also be over five cities'."*
>
> — Luke 19:17-19

Question #1: I want to be an informed citizen, but how can I get good information on candidates? How can I know how they will vote when they get in office?

Numerous sites provide excellent information on candidates running for office, including ChristianVoterGuide.com. But there are times when some of the races or candidates on your ballot may not be listed on some voters guides. In such cases, it is easy to create your own, and many citizens now do this. Lesson #11 identifies key issues in God's "Top Ten," so you can take those issues, such as abortion, traditional marriage, and the public acknowledgment of God, and contact your local candidates and ask them where they stand on these issues, as well as on other issues that may be of interest to you, including local tax or policy issues. Or you might contact someone you know who has a Biblical worldview and who is active in the political arena and ask them about the candidates. After you do your research, it is simple to create a voter guide that places candidates side by side, showing where each stands on the various issues that you examined. Then distribute your findings to your neighbors, church, and others in your sphere of influence, including posting it on various social media accounts.

Significantly, modern experience shows that there is one particular issue that is an extremely accurate indicator of how a candidate will vote on nearly every other important issue, regardless of whether those votes occur at the local, state, or federal levels.

Recall that Lesson #2 identified the five principles upon which American government was based. The first three were: (1) The official acknowledgment of a Divine Creator; (2) the recognition that the Creator gives certain inalienable or natural rights to man; and (3) the affirmation that government exists primarily for the purpose of protecting those inalienable rights.

13 SESSION

STUDY GUIDE

Affirming this, Samuel Adams, the "Father of the American Revolution," declared that "Government . . . was originally designed for the preservation of the unalienable rights," and also noted that those inalienable rights included "first, a right to life; secondly, to liberty; thirdly, to property." Other Founders made similar pronouncements, but notice that the right to life was the first of the inalienable rights that government was to protect.

Today, we wrongly assume that the Founders were not talking about the abortion issue, but they did indeed specifically address that issue. After all, the Bible tells us in Ecclesiastes 1:9 that there is nothing new under the sun; and as long as there have been pregnancies, there were those who did not want to be pregnant and who sought to end the pregnancy. Abortion is nothing new: it is the technology used to perform it that differs from generation to generation.

Founder James Wilson, a signer of both the Declaration and the Constitution, spoke very clearly about this issue. Placed by President George Washington as an original justice on the U. S. Supreme Court, Wilson started the first organized legal training in America. Concerning abortion, he told law students:

> With consistency, beautiful and undeviating, human life, from its commencement to its close, is protected by the Common Law. In the contemplations of law, life begins when the infant is first able to stir in the womb. By the law, [that] life is protected.

American law and public policy was clear: as soon as it was known that there was life in the womb, that life, right then and there, was protected by the Common Law, which the Founders officially recognized in the Seventh Amendment to the Constitution. Back in their day, it might take weeks before it could be known for sure that life was indeed present in the womb, but now with our modern technology we can know with certainty within only a few days. But regardless of how long it took, as soon as it was known that unborn life was present, from that point forward that unborn life was to be protected. As an elderly John Quincy Adams reminded the rising generation:

> Ask the Declaration of Independence and that will tell you that its authors held for self-evident truth that the right to life is the first of the unalienable rights of man [and] to secure and not to destroy it governments are instituted among men.

Across much of Europe at that time (and now across much of America today), it was wrongly believed that parents gave life to children; so under the law in those countries, parents had the right to take their child's life. But Americans knew that the life of a child came not from parents but rather from God, so parents therefore had no right to deprive an unborn child of his or her life. As signer of the Declaration John Witherspoon acknowledged:

> Some nations have given parents the power of life and death over their children... [In America,] we have denied the power of life and death to parents.

So the right to life was considered the first of the inalienable rights. And modern experience repeatedly proves that if a government leader is willing to violate the first and foremost of all inalienable rights (i.e., the right to life), then he or she likely will also disregard other God-given rights.

Thus, if he does not support the inalienable right to life, he will almost certainly be wrong on the government protecting the inalienable right to worship God according to the dictates of conscience from the First Amendment, or the inalienable right of self-defense in the Second Amendment, or the inalienable right to be safe from governmental intrusion into our "persons, houses, papers, and effects" as guaranteed in the Fourth Amendment, or the inalienable right of private property protection as secured in the Fifth Amendment, and so forth. In short, if a leader does not protect the first of all inalienable rights, then experience proves that all our other individual rights are also frequently at risk from that leader.

Of course, we are often told by political pundits that voters really don't care about such "social issues" such as abortion or marriage or religious rights but rather that they care only about economic things such as debt, spending, taxation, jobs, and so forth. Let's pretend for a moment that economics is all that matters in public policy.

In every session of Congress, from ten to thirteen thousand bills are introduced, and Congressmen cast hundreds of votes. If all you care about are economic issues, then you should check the congressional scorecards compiled by various economic watchdog groups. Such groups don't care a whit about the Second Amendment, or religious liberties, or private property, or abortion, or marriage, or any other "social issue." All they do is monitor, record, and report on the hundreds of economic votes that a Congressman casts every session of Congress. These economic groups then rank all 435 Members of the House, and all 100 Members of the Senate, from the 100 percent-ers all the way down to the 0 percent-ers.

But if you take those economic voting scorecards and lay them down side by side with the scorecards produced by the various national pro-life groups who rank the Congressmen according to their votes on the life issue, you will find that those Congressmen who are the best in defending the unalienable right to life nearly always have the best voting record on economic issues. Likewise, those who are most pro-abortion are the ones with the worst voting record on economic issues.

It might sound strange that where a Congressman is on the protection of unborn life is one of the best indicators of where he or she will be on economic issues, but it actually makes perfect sense. After all, if a leader won't protect your life, why would he protect your money? — your life is much more important than your money. This principle of protecting life first holds true with leaders at every level, including at the state, regional, county, and local level.

Once you determine where a candidate (whether president, governor, mayor, school board president, or dogcatcher) is on the protection of unborn life, you can usually accurately predict how they will vote on virtually every other significant or constitutional issue. If they won't protect the first and most important of our inalienable rights, then they are unlikely to protect the rest of them in their votes and public policies.

Question #2: I want to believe that Christians like me can make a difference at the polls, but there are times when my vote feels insignificant. Is there any correlation between the degree of Christian participation and the outcome of an election?

You may not feel significant or that your one vote makes any difference, and thus you may not vote or do anything else political. After all, what is just one vote? But the problem is that millions of American Christians are thinking the same thing you are, and like you, millions of them do not cast their one vote — meaning that millions of individual votes are not being cast, one vote at a time. Consider some facts on this.

More than nine out of ten residents of the United States who are 18 or older have the right to vote, but less than three out of every four register to do so. And in presidential elections, when turnout is highest among registered voters, one quarter of these three-out-of-four don't bother to cast a ballot — at all. Thus, four out of every ten adults who are qualified to participate in the process voluntarily refuse to do so. In recent presidential elections, this means that up to 90 million adults who were qualified to vote made an individual conscious decision not to do so; and among Evangelicals, the number routinely runs between 30 and 40 million who did not vote. When you take into consideration the fact that recent presidential candidates have been decided by relatively slim margins of only a few percentage points, the mathematics became a bit disturbing. The bottom line is that with just six out of ten qualified adults bothering to register and vote, and the victorious candidate drawing support from about

13 SESSION

STUDY GUIDE

half of the sixty percent, our nation is regularly being led by presidents who have the backing of less than one-third of the adult population. Too many Christians believe that their vote doesn't make any difference and thus by the tens of millions they sit on the sidelines.

Voter turnout is even worse in non-presidential election years (called off-year elections), when only thirty-nine percent of the two-thirds of registered Americans vote. This means that in non-presidential elections, only about one-in-four Americans vote to choose their federal congressmen and senators, and state legislators and governors. And since only a majority of that one-fourth is necessary to select the winners, this means that essentially seven out of eight Americans do not vote for those who become their governors, senators, and representatives.

In local elections, the turnout number is usually down in the two to four percent turnout range. In fact, a candidate who won the mayor's race in America's second largest city, after spending more than $19 million and participating in 40 public debates, declared: "I got 33% of the 20% turnout of the 49% of the population registered to vote. I had a landslide with 2.6% of the population."

There are countless statistics documenting that when Christian voter turnout increases, the quality of the candidates who get elected correspondingly improves. This is especially the case when Christians vote their values. Sadly, if just the currently registered Evangelicals showed up to vote (not counting the tens of millions of Evangelicals who are not registered to vote), there would be no culture war in America today. So any feeling of whether or not your vote makes a difference is irrelevant. You must vote because it is your duty to do so, regardless of how you personally feel and regardless of what you think will be the outcome. Our negative attitude towards voting and political involvement too often becomes self-fulfilling prophecy.

"When the righteous are in authority, the people rejoice; But when a wicked man rules, the people groan."

— Proverbs 29:2

SESSION 13
STUDY GUIDE

ADDITIONAL READING/VIEWING/LISTENING

- *Biblical Principles and the Political Process* by David Barton
- *U-Turn* by David Barton and George Barna
- *A Nation Adrift* by Timothy Barton
- *Original Intent* by David Barton

DISCUSSION QUESTIONS AFTER WATCHING THE VIDEO

1. Is it a Christian's responsibility to be politically active even if it doesn't do any good?

Yes. As Founders such as John Quincy Adams believed, "Duty is ours, results are God's." You will not answer to God for who got elected, or how well that person governs while holding office. Rather, you will answer to God for whether or not you cast your vote (that is, whether you participated in the stewardship He gave you over your community, state, and nation) and also for whom you cast your vote — whether you supported a friend or enemy of Biblical values. If Christians across America would simply do what is Biblically right without trying to predict the results or effectiveness of their vote or involvement, the nation would turn in a righteous direction much more rapidly. After all, for decades, almost three-fourths of the nation has self-identified as "Christian," but most refuse to be salt or light. Yet regardless of what any other Christian does, you must do what is right. In John 21, Peter complained to Jesus about the behavior of another disciple, to which Jesus pointedly replied: "What does that matter to you? You follow Me" (v. 22). This is how we should look at our voting. You must vote, regardless of what anyone else does, and you must do so every time you have opportunity, no matter how insignificant or inconsequential you might consider that vote or election to be.

2. Which is more important: fiscal issues or social issues?

Proverbs 14:34 reminds us that "Righteousness exalts a nation, but sin is a reproach to any people," and most often today, issues of Biblical righteousness are classified as part of social rather than economic policy. Thus, from a Biblical perspective, social policy usually trumps fiscal policy. Furthermore, the direction of fiscal policy nearly always follows the direction of social policy — that is, if the social culture begins to turn downward, its economics will usually follow, and when the social culture is strong, the economy is nearly always strong. The right to life is the first among our God-given inalienable rights and it is at the core of Biblical standards of righteousness, and if the right to life is disregarded or abrogated by any candidate, it is likely that no other policy will be sound, including economic ones.

3. How can you get involved in the civic arena?

- Vote in all primaries, elections, and referendums
- Research candidates so you can cast informed votes
- Identify good voters guides, and if you can't find one, then create one for the races that appear on your ballot
- Distribute voter guides at churches and to other supportive groups or individuals

NOTES

NOTES

NOTES

NOTES